EOGHAN CORRY is 24 and h... Sunday Tribune since 1980. ... award for young journalists in ... Barry McGuigan. His centenary ... Kildare GAA was published in 1984.

McGUIGAN

THE UNAUTHORISED BIOGRAPHY

Eoghan Corry

MAGILL

Published by Magill Publications Ltd
14 Merrion Row Dublin 2.

First edition September 1985

Copyright © Eoghan Corry

Cover design by Robert Armstrong

All photographs: Pacemaker

Printed by Irish Printers Ltd

Distributed by Newspread Ltd

ISBN 0.9507659.4.5

ACKNOWLEDGEMENTS

Thank you to all who helped piece this offering together.

To Gerry Callan, for boxing expertise and spadework in delving through the intricacies of the McGuigan and Eastwood story.

To Rita Byrne who worked day and night typesetting the book.

To Gene Kerrigan who edited the manuscript.

To Deirdre Purcell, Nicky Kelly, John Waters and Steve Ryan for editorial help.

To Pat Pidgeon, Alwyn Gillespie and Barbara Nolan, who laid out Barry McGuigan in double-quick time.

To Michael McGeary and the Irish News, *Sean Kilfeather, Hugh Russell, Eddy Thompson, Martin Brereton, Mick Holmes, Ferdie Pacheco, Bobby McQuillar, Rick Young, Rick Gentile, Alex Wallec and others too numerous to mention who reminisced about their times with McGuigan.*

To Vincent Browne who published the book and won the arguments.

To Eileen Pearson who organised us all.

To the staff in Maynooth College Library.

Eoghan Corry

Contents

CHAPTER 1: THE LOFTUS HEIGHTS   13
1. Pedroza
2. Weigh-in
3. Here We Go . . .
4. The Fight
5. "You are a great champion . . ."

CHAPTER 2: CHAMPION NO. 22   23
1. The Stuff Of Legends
2. Ups And Downs
3. Might Have Beens
4. New York And The Future
5. The Champ
6. Old Score

CHAPTER 3: INTO THE RING   47
1. Boxing School
2. Bobbing And Weaving
3. Medals
4. Disappointments

CHAPTER 4: THE PRO GAME   67
1. Young Man In A Hurry
2. Barney Eastwood
3. Marketing Mr Nice Guy
4. Victories And Defeats
5. Bum-A-Month
6. Fists Of Fate
7. Trauma
8. The Punch
9. Double Crisis

CHAPTER 5: HERO   95
   1. The British Title
   2. A Bridge To The South
   3. America
   4. Back To Europe
   5. Fighting Nati
   6. "There's no point in reaching for the ceiling."
   7. The Stick
   8. Caba
   9. Breaking Into TV
   10. The Amachewer
   11. Orozco
   12. "Leave the fighting to McGuigan . . ."
   13. "Try not to be a wally."
   14. The Ghost

CHAPTER 6: CHASING A CHAMPION   139
   1. Laporte In Ten
   2. Contender
   3. Reaction
   4. Options
   5. Gentlemanly Conduct
   6. The Cost
   7. Old Friends
   8. Press Conference
   9. Hero's Welcome
   10. Big Bucks
   11. White Hope
   12. Home Town

APPENDIX 1 – Boxing: The Medical Facts   169
APPENDIX 2 – Champions   177
APPENDIX 3 – The Irish Champions   182
APPENDIX 4 – Irish-American World Champions   190

The beginning of the end of Eusebio Pedroza's reign as Featherweight champion of the World as he falls victim to McGuigan's pre-planned right hook.

Moments of madness as the referee Stan Christodoulo holds back McGuigan. Pedroza looks decidedly groggy as he begins an instinctive climb back to his feet.

Satisfaction on the face of the Clones Cyclone as he turns away from the scene.

McGuigan's Pro Record

Born: February 28, 1961

DATE	OPPONENT	SITE	RESULT
		1981	
May 10	Selvin Bell	Dublin	KO2
June 20	Gary Lucas	London	KO4
Aug 3	Peter Eubanks	Brighton	L8
Sept 22	Jean Marc Renard	Belfast	W8
Oct 26	Terry Pizzaro	Belfast	KO4
Dec 8	Peter Eubanks	Belfast	KO8
		1982	
Jan 27	Luis de la Sagra	Belfast	W8
Feb 8	Ian Murray	London	KO3
Feb 23	Angel Oliver	Belfast	KO3
Mar 23	Angelo Licata	Belfast	KO2
Apr 22	Gary Lucas	Enniskillen	KO1
June 12	Young Ali	London	KO6
Oct 5	Jimmy Duncan	Belfast	KO5
Nov 9	Paul Huggins	Belfast	KO5
		1983	
Apr 12	Vernon Penprase	Belfast	KO2
	(Won Vacant British Title)		
May 22	Sammy Meck	Navan	KO6
July 9	Lavon McGowan	Chicago	KO1
Oct 5	Ruben Herasme	Belfast	KO2
Nov 16	Valerio Nati	Belfast	KO6
	(Won Vacant European Title)		

1984

Jan 25	Charm Chiteule	Belfast	KO10
Apr 4	Jose Caba	Belfast	KO7
June 5	Esteban Eguia	Kensington	KO3

(Retained European Title)

June 30	Paul De Vorce	Belfast	KO5
Oct 13	Felipe Orozco	Belfast	KO2
Dec 19	Clyde Ruan	Belfast	KO4

(Retained British and European Titles)

1985

Feb 23	Juan LaPorte	Belfast	W10
Mar 26	Farid Gallouze	London	KO2

(Retained European Title)

June 8	Eusebio Pedroza	London	W15

(Won WBA Featherweight Title)

SUMMARY

BOUTS	WINS	LOSSES	DRAWS	KOs
28	27	1	0	23

"You can forget about it," Barney Eastwood threatens to withdraw McGuigan at the weigh-in stage.

The scene of the World championship fight, Loftus Road, is a soccer stadium normally used by Queens Park Rangers club.

CHAPTER 1

The Loftus Heights

"I knew he was knackered. I could see it in his eyes."
— Barry McGuigan, WBA Featherweight champion of the world, on his defeat of one of the great modern champions, Eusebio Pedroza.

1. Pedroza

Reigning world featherweight champion Eusebio Pedroza was angry. Throughout the week before his contest with Irish challenger Barry McGuigan in London he complained. Or at least his manager Santiago Del Rio said enough to keep the countless morning and evening newspapers in copy.

The coverage had been hostile. These Latin Americans are always complaining, you know . . . patronising sort of stuff. Pedroza came to London with a reputation for foul play. His opponent of January 1982, Juan Laporte, claimed that Pedroza had thrown fourteen low blows and twenty-five kidney punches among fifty-eight fouls committed in their championship fight. Use of elbows, shoulders and other dirty tricks were all written into Pedroza's flawed pedigree.

Much more significant were the facts that he had not been marketed successfully enough to make money from American television; that he had the distraction of a political career in Panama; and that he was aging. He was more than the official age of twenty-nine (born on March 2nd

1956) and even according to some, already thirty-two years old. There were major changes in style, the open attacking stance of his younger days after he first won the title by knocking out Spaniard Cecilio Lastra in April 1978 was no more. The punching power was no longer sufficient to knock opponents out (he had twenty-four in his 39-3-1 record). The style was much tighter.

Patience and stamina were his trademarks. He knew that the last five rounds were championship territory. McGuigan had never been past ten rounds before.

He also had major weight problems. When he came to London for the McGuigan European title defence against Farid Gallouze in March, Pedroza was twenty-three pounds over the featherweight limit. He liked the good lifestyle, and was well known for blowing up between fights. He also took no prisoners when he was out of his boxing shorts. He once fired a shot at someone he thought was trying to rob his sportscar in Panama City, wounding him.

The appointment of referee Stan Christodoulo of South Africa for the contest drew the first salvo of controversy. Christodoulo had handled the fifteen-round contest between Pedroza and Jose Caba in April 1983, had warned Pedroza six times but did not take any other action. The British press took that as a definite sign that the referee was pro-Pedroza.

The next controversy was over weight. Raphael Ramos Yordan, the official World Boxing Association supervisor arrived in London on the Wednesday before the fight and complained that the fighters had not yet had a trial weigh-in. So it was arranged for early the following day. The press announced it gleefully, howling that Pedroza would never make the weight.

The weigh-in on Thursday morning was confrontational. The fighters glared at one another, but the situation was defused when they exchanged thumbs-up signs. McGuigan even managed a "how're ye doing" amid the hostile glares. Pedroza made the weight by a full pound. News hounds were visibly disappointed.

Pedroza's next move was to get the ring extended from eighteen-foot square to twenty-foot square. The technicians from Wembley stadium, from whom the ring was borrowed, worked on the extension when the ring was installed in Loftus Road.

Pedroza was following the old adage that the "Big ring is a boxer's ring, the small ring is a fighter's ring."

The overall perception of Pedroza before the fight was of the boxer's boxer, full of craft, experience, and unspectacular skill. He was matched against the youthful, exuberant, McGuigan. The fighter against the crafty, dirty old dog.

* * * * * * *

2. Weigh-in

Finbarr Patrick McGuigan started his most important day in the company of two of his closest friends, Sean McGivern from Bangor and his fifteen-year-old brother-in-law Ross Mealiff.

Mealiff had been asked if he would like to be in the World champion's corner by manager Barney Eastwood. He was delighted to accept.

Through the training he had stayed close to Barry, helping, calming, staying with McGuigan.

McGuigan rose at 7.45am for a preliminary check on his weight. He was comfortably under the limit. With a week to go McGuigan was nervous. With a day to go he was less so. He was relaxed on the morning of the World title fight.

For two and a quarter hours he dehydrated. He made his way from the Holiday Inn to the Odeon Cinema, at the Haymarket, stopping for a flask of coffee and some Mars bars. Already the fans were congregating at the cinema. Some of them brought their massive banners. They chanted and cheered for McGuigan, their hero.

The weigh-in was the scene of the last dramatic burst of fire in the psychological war. In front of television cameras, well within the evening paper newspaper deadlines and the one o'clock lunchtime bulletins, Eastwood threatened to withdraw McGuigan from the title fight.

Pedroza, too, had weighed in, unofficially, before the title fight. He had come to the Odeon for a trial at eight in the morning, the time initially suggested for the weigh-in by his manager, Santiago Del Rio. He had made the nine stone limit, then returned for the official weigh-in at ten. There were already 500 chanting McGuigan fans in the cinema.

It is traditional for the challenger to weigh-in first. McGuigan was nowhere to be seen. The fans saw Pedroza and chanted louder. *Barr-eee, Barr-eee.* The Panamanian scrambled through the assembled boxing bureaucrats, stepped on to the scales, and dismounted five seconds later. The scales still buzzed and were unsteady, but the McGuigan fans had seen their favourite entering on the right hand side of the stage and had begun to cheer him. Pedroza was off the scales, the World Boxing Association representative, Puerto Rican Ramos Yordan, was happy, and even the gesticulating promoter, Stephen Eastwood, could do nothing about it.

But Eastwood tried. He swept his hands apart in disagreement. The fans sensed a row. They chanted and stopped chanting in one breath. Racing across the stage came the burly figure of B.J.Eastwood, like an actor who had been just an instant late for his cue. And he was angry.

"I never saw Pedroza weigh in," he shouted. He remonstrated with Mickey Duff and Mr Yordan.

"I want him on the scales again. McGuigan is not getting on the scales until Pedroza gets up again." The media men sensed melodrama. "Poppycock," the WBA man seemed to say.

Eastwood insisted that there be another weigh-in. "Unless there is one in half an hour you can forget about it." A real threat, but the WBA man was not impressed. He was used to the pre-fight hype, and not amused by it any more. Everybody else in the packed cinema was enjoying the bonus. "If that's the sort of fair play we get tonight," Eastwood said, "you forget about it." Still no impression on Yordan. Eventually Eastwood announced to the partisans in the cinema "I'm disappointed with the World Boxing Association and with the British Boxing Board of Control, but we're going ahead."

Point made. Sighs of relief. The whole incident had lasted just long enough for an airing on the lunch-time bulletins. It had been dramatic and fast-moving. No editing was necessary.

Everybody clapped. McGuigan came over to the scales. Master of ceremonies Danny Small announced that he weighed in at eight stone, thirteen pounds, fourteen ounces — two ounces under the limit.

Pedroza tried to make his way backstage but was confronted by a dozen chanting fans. *Barr-eee, Barr-eee.* He was not intimidated. He put on his mean pre-fight glare face and sneered back at them. Then he left the cinema.

A police decision banning banners in the ground was relayed. "He will do the fighting, not you," the spokesman said hopefully. "We're not here for trouble, we're here for a good fight."

After that it was back to the hostelries.

* * * * * * *

3. Here We Go . . .

McGuigan likes to sleep on the afternoon of a World title fight. He came back to the Holiday Inn with all his weight worries over, tucked into bacon and sausage and eggs, and headed out for a brisk walk. It was a risky business in the streets of London, with so many keyed up fans around, but McGuigan stayed away from Edgeware Road and the main thoroughfares around the hotel. Nobody recognised the prospective champion.

Being with McGuigan on the day of a fight is a cheerful experience. He likes to relax a lot, talk about things other than boxing, play cards (he cheats) and trade jokes.

McGuigan liked the joke about the blind man who was walking down the street when a dog piddled against his leg. The man took out a biscuit and gave it to the dog. A passer-by was puzzled and asked him why. "So as I'll know to kick it at the other end."

There was no rest for McGuigan, he could not sleep. At 3.30 he had more carbohydrates, and tucked into cheesecake.

McGuigan was as relaxed as he has ever been on the day of the fight. But inside there was a slow-building tension. He travelled to the Queens Park Rangers soccer ground by team bus. Inside he began the slow build up, removed from the crowd, talking a little. He prayed.

Earlier that week, strict Catholic Pedroza said: "He who is with God will win." McGuigan too is a strict Catholic.

Usually, McGuigan sums up his dressing room experience with: "I say a wee prayer and I try to relax." Prayer and Santiago Del Rio dominated his pre-fight moments.

The dreaded Panamanian manager arrived in the dressing room just as McGuigan had oiled his body — what he calls putting his war-paint on — and had bandaged his hands. Del Rio wanted all the bandages off. Start again! Eastwood shouted a lot at him. The WBA supervisor said he was happy with the bandaging. But in the end McGuigan had to take them all off, and bandage higher towards the knuckles. "Do it again," said Del Rio. The boxer burst into tears.

McGuigan is moved to tears very easily. This was his last outburst before the big fight. The hands were re-bandaged. It was time to wipe away tears, and to concentrate on looking mean.

Show-business likes to tap emotions and bottle them for public consumption. Boxing, show-business with blood, succeeds more than most. The moments before a boxer begins his trek to the ringside, with chanting crowds all around, are emotional.

Every boxer gets the Rocky fanfare in his home town. On June 8, London was Barry McGuigan's home town.

The fans could not even hear the Rocky theme music. That part of the emotional build-up was confined to living rooms invaded by television.

Somewhere in the chaotic passage from the dressing rooms to the ring at the centre of the board-covered football pitch could be seen a moving flag-pole with McGuigan's personal blue flag of peace, a dove, a boxing glove and a pacifist statement crowded onto it. Behind it moved a spotlight. Somewhere somebody was operating the spotlight, pretty sure that if he shone it a few yards behind the flag he would find the young boxer that 25,000 fans had come to see. Maybe. Nobody saw whether or not the spotlight was on target.

On the living room television set, some of the ringside faces were recognisable in the confusion.

The family . . .

B.J. Eastwood . . . Barney to his family, B.J. to his friends and acquaintances, Mr Eastwood to boxer McGuigan, who believes that he should have respect for his elders. An image of benevolence as the millionaire boxer who adopted McGuigan. Now stout and balding and snarling and clad in white robes he led the way as the bouncers tried to clear a path.

Paddy Byrne . . . the best cut-man in Europe, McGuigan's match-maker (when he needed one), McGuigan's adviser (when he needed one), Eastwood's agent (when he needed one), an unpretentious regular at World championship ringsides. Looking cool and calm as befits a veteran of these occasions. Looking like he desperately wanted to win this one.

Eddie Shaw . . . the Belfast boxing trainer brought from amateur obscurity to world fame by the prowess of his protege McGuigan. The man who turned down an offer to move to Chicago, because his family would not like the life over there.

Somewhere down there was Barry McGuigan.

The boxing supporters were in a soccer stadium. They sang their soccer song, *Here we go . . . Here we go . . .* ad nauseum. And they chanted this mantra-like, waiting to go, waiting to go, waiting to go.

And in oil and blue and yellow robe McGuigan climbed into the ring.

There were those that objected to the British National anthem. The McGuigan juxtapostion of nationality and religion and reality struck again. Pompously, they called "let ye all be upstanding for the National Anthem" . . . *God save our noble Queen* . . . song of division in Ireland.

But this was London. The British anthem could only be heard at the ringside seats. Those on the terraces, a hundred yards or so away from the distant figures in the ring, were not even aware it had been played.

If *God Save The Queen* had not been heard, there was no chance at all that the Panamanian National Anthem would be. The formalities were not over, although the boxers were in an imperilled position, stripped and robed. They could easily lose vital body heat that would affect their highly tuned muscles in the Saturday night breeze. They danced and feinted. Pedroza looked glazed and tense.

Some of those dress-suited characters in the ring turned around to try to halt the tumultuous *Here we go* . . . Here we most certainly did not go. They had lined up a last pre-match punch in the tearducts. Pat McGuigan, father of Barry, singer and record artiste, missed the opening line of Danny Boy in the noise. He started ". . . and down the mountain side." The opening line of Danny Boy was not important. Somehow the word trickled through the terraces that there was singing to be done. *The Derry Air*, symbol of Northern Ireland, to be joined in an emotional high, just at the high part, the rest did not matter . . .

"But come ye back when summer's in the meadow.
Or when the valley's hushed and white with snow,
'Tis I'll be there in sunshine or in sorrow . . ."

"Barry, Barry, We Love You" they chanted. Introductions, an Irish Leprechaun danced in gaudy green on the stage, and the whole damned WBA World Championship racket was unveiled before the eyes of 25,000 paying spectators, eighteen million British and Irish viewers, countless others with junk-food TV-lunchpacks some 3,000 miles away, and even farther. TV viewers in twelve countries.

They had talked about Pedroza -v- McGuigan for eighteen months now. Was it only eighteen months?

* * * * * * *

4. The Fight

McGuigan was not to know that aggression would sway the judges from the start, that he would win even the three first rounds, which were legitimately Pedroza's because of his text-book punching, knuckle part of the glove on the target, jab, jab, jab, consistently and firmly as he retreated.

Instead, even the judges were caught with the fever of the night. Ove Oveson of Denmark made it 149-139, referee Stan Christodoulo 148-138, and Venezuelan judge Fernando Viso 147-140.

There were three distinct phases in this World title fight. The most astounding was the first — which comprised the opening six and a half rounds, in which the pace was so astonishingly fast and furious that most observers decided the fight would not go the full distance. From the seventh to the twelfth McGuigan looked more and more capable of the knockout punch that would end the contest, and the more dangerous he looked the more likely Pedroza was to come back and win a round. In the third phase, Pedroza's legs had given, and he was fighting with experience and instinct, waiting for his last desperate chance — a moment of over-enthusiasm by the younger fighter.

One . . .

McGuigan started aggressively. That was what expected. It was expected that aggression would burn him out. Instead it burned out Pedroza.

In the first, McGuigan scored with a good right to the head. He bobbed Pedroza against the corner late in the round when the champion moved his head to avoid a jab. McGuigan was worried about his left elbow as he jabbed. Every time he snapped it, which was about four times in this round alone, it was like someone was sticking needles in his elbow. Pedroza retreated rapidly, never putting a foot out of place, shoulders swaying gently, counter-punching shrewdly, hips locked into place, forearms and gloves sliding upwards and back down to frustrate McGuigan's jab. He jabbed effectively with his left, occasionally crossing with his right. Pedroza hit low. McGuigan retaliated. Pedroza was boohed for using his head.

Two...

In the second a blow to Pedroza's ribs staggered the champion, but only through imbalance. McGuigan was carefully avoiding committing himself. He scored well with lefts to the body, and bobbed Pedroza to the ropes with twenty seconds to go. McGuigan stood at the centre of the ring. He used the space to force Pedroza outwards to the ropes, then wheeled after him, rotating on his own axis. And he was caught. A right from the champion reminded him of the dangers of leading with the traditional left. By the end of the round McGuigan's face had been reddened by Pedroza's constant, threatening, jab, jab, jab.

McGuigan was waiting for the chance to use his right, an old failing returned. When he threw it, it tended to go way over the top.

Three...

In the third McGuigan cornered Pedroza twice, but was called by the referee for low punching. He proved over-eager to come in and score with lefts to the head. Pedroza was stunned with a right to the ribs when the champion had been cornered and used his forearms to cover his head, McGuigan landed three aggressively strong punches towards the end of the round. Both boxers ended the round crouching in the centre of the ring.

Pedroza was scoring, precisely and efficiently. Many observers gave him each of the first three rounds. The judges did not. The first effective bolo punch came in the third from Pedroza. He appeared to have sustained damage over the left eye. But if boxing excellence counted for anything, he should have been ahead.

Four...

The fourth saw the first sign of McGuigan's relentless pressure paying off. Yet Pedroza was unmoved by a whacking great left to the head. Pedroza's efforts to tie up McGuigan were not succeeding. Then McGuigan ran into a left that snapped back his head and sent water and sweat flying back into the cold night air. Twice Pedroza staggered. Once Pedroza's head was adjudged low. But Pedroza was slowing down. McGuigan was becoming more and more confident. The sheer volume of his punching was telling.

Five . . .

Then, Bang! McGuigan's left ligament was defused. He had let the explosive left off its leash, run into trouble, taken a colossal right to the body. And paid the price. He had snapped his elbow, all the needles had been injected at once.

"Don't let it annoy you," Eastwood told him in the corner. "You can beat this man with one hand." So for ten rounds, McGuigan was one-handed, unable to throw two big ones in succession. It may have prevented him being trapped by the cagey Pedroza. As the fifth had ended, Pedroza threw an uppercut after the bell. It may have been frustration. It looked much, much more like confidence.

Six . . .

Pedroza was closing down McGuigan, an increasingly confident McGuigan, more and more in the sixth. McGuigan was checked for use of his head. He also had a successful left to the head but did not get enough power behind it. The explosive left looked defused. Six rounds over, McGuigan aggressive, Pedroza consistent.

Seven . . .

In the seventh it was time something happened to the fight's breathless pace. Pedroza had not had a rest round, and it was clear that he was becoming unhappy with the course the fight was taking. In the seventh and eighth he stepped up the volume of his own punches. It was his turn to effect pressure and to use this half-way stage of the fight to start taking control. He could hardly have suspected that the judges had already marked him so hopelessly behind.

He was beginning to dominate for the first two minutes of the seventh round. McGuigan sensed this and worried that he had not put on enough pressure in those opening six rounds.

But Pedroza's laid-back, low guard was dropping even further as the champion set to work. Pedroza depends on his ability to get his tall, erect head out of the way of any punches that find their way over the guard. McGuigan was punching off-target. He dropped the left a little too low.

McGuigan saw the opening.

Nine weeks of practice paid off. Nine weeks with Gerald Hayes, dropping the left, being caught by the dummy left and clunked with the powerful punch to the right — the pride of McGuigan's amateur days — and start all over again. From McGuigan's perspective, nine weeks of seeing the opening, dummying, scoring and stepping back.

The punch came with two minutes and eighteen seconds of the seventh round gone. It changed irrevocably the course of the fight.

Nine weeks of practice, blinded by the left, clunked by the right, Pedroza hit the canvas by bobbing off the second and bottom ropes, taking another left hook on the way down.

The 25,000 screamed, the referee shouted the numbers emotionally, his face watching first McGuigan, then Pedroza, grimacing. Two . . . three. Pedroza had started rising as soon as he hit the canvas, he was now back on his feet, looking a little dazed, a little bored by the whole ceremonial. Four . . . five . . . six . . . There was one more second's respite when the eight had sounded. Then McGuigan set about the chase.

A right misses. A left misses, but only just. A right misses. A left misses. Pedroza is retreating, McGuigan committing himself over-anxiously to the big one. All the champion can do is clutch for McGuigan's shoulders. A left veers towards Pedroza's shoulders but the head instinctively moves back to safety. Pedroza stalls and tries a left jab of his own. Then a McGuigan left hook finds the champion's face. Back into trouble.

Pedroza has now turned to retreat back across the ring, looking for the open space, avoiding the ropes and corners. He ducks to avoid a right then squares up, forcing McGuigan to defend himself. McGuigan draws a weak jab then fires another left hook that makes contact. McGuigan feigns a left to the body but Pedroza smothers the subsequent right. The boxers are now inches apart. McGuigan tries another left to the chin. Pedroza retreats just in time. A cracking right to the chin. Pedroza is almost felled again. A left is just too low. Pedroza tries an instinctive, retaliatory left. He drops his guard. McGuigan scores again. Pedroza ducks. Clang. As McGuigan's right flies in again the bell goes to end the hunt. Pedroza raises both fists in the air in empty defiance as McGuigan turns back to his corner.

Eight . . .

From his corner, Pedroza stared into the crowd, expressionless. He reckoned McGuigan's exuberance would leave him vulnerable. Restore the volume of his punching and he could get through.

And so, in the eighth, Pedroza's resilience was seen again. Far from being dazed he was right back into action. McGuigan's head was snapped back twice in rapid succession. The spray sailed through the night air again. McGuigan also took a solid right round the back of the head. The bolo shot was back in action.

Pedroza too, was back in action. He outboxed McGuigan for two of the three minutes at the start of the eighth. Around the ground the pundits pondered the mark of a real champion. Champions recover from set-backs, like Pedroza was doing. Real champions can take it.

So could McGuigan. Pedroza met his aggressor and forced him backwards, but the man who had forced the pace of the first six rounds was chirpily taking everything, aware that the pendulum was now moving if not coming to the other side, aware that Pedroza's confidence would grow if he showed any signs of flinching.

Nine . . .

McGuigan ran into a right early on in the ninth. But a right of his own shifted the round back in his favour. It came ten seconds from the end of the round. Another chase, this time just ten seconds long, ensued. "Jesus, every time I hit him it seemed to be at the end of a round," McGuigan mourned afterwards.

McGuigan had been worried about the seventh and eighth rounds, about how he had not kept up the pressure on the champion. If he got him again, he vowed, he would keep rushing at him.

The ten seconds at the end of the eighth were not enough, but they did seriously affect Pedroza. Even at the start of the ninth he had not recovered. The initial right caused

Pedroza to stagger backwards. McGuigan tried to steady Pedroza's head with his left to set it up for a blow with the right, but the champion took a vital step backwards. Pedroza then smothered two lefts and probably evaded another right before he ran out of luck and was caught with two left hooks that caused him to lean back precariously for an instant. But Pedroza stayed on his feet and did not take a count.

McGuigan may have appeared over-anxious. He let in three big punches, two lefts and a right, after the bell. McGuigan felt there was still about thirty seconds to go. In the din, it is likely that neither McGuigan nor the referee heard the bell.

Ten . . .

The tenth had warning signs all over it for Pedroza. Fatigue. "I knew he was knackered," McGuigan said afterwards. "I could see it in his eyes."

Pedroza slipped early in the round. His legs were failing. This looked like it was going to be a test of durability. Paradoxically, he finished stronger than he started. Pedroza passed the test.

McGuigan was now feeling the handicap of not being able to jab. He was told to hit with the right, then bring a left hook either to the body or head. So he had to feign the jab, throw the right and then try the left hook. It was important to let them go in rapid succession once Pedroza had been hit. No big punch at the back of the punch. No fancy work. Just a right and then a left hook. McGuigan understood. But there was no way through.

Eleven . . .

The eleventh ended, and still Pedroza stood. McGuigan still grows frustrated at the memory of not having put him away. Right, then left hook, and be careful.

Pedroza had banked on scoring his way back into contention in the fight, although he was now feeling the effects of the early pace. He was succeeding remarkably well. In both the eleventh and twelfth Pedroza started the round well but faded quickly. His tiredness showed when he lost his balance after two minutes of the eleventh.

Pedroza was delaying, delaying blatantly, more and

more at the start of each round. But McGuigan too was looking tired. Not comparatively tired — Pedroza was hanging on for dear life — just tired enough to fall into old characteristic weaknesses. A right uppercut that went too high, occasional thrust to the left when he threw a strong left jab, leg stance too wide . . . not crucial, when you are winning a World championship fight.

Twelve . . .

The twelfth showed Pedroza's elbows in action. Those gigantic forearms were shielding, McGuigan had fewer body punches, and the round was very scrappy as a result. It was quite possible Pedroza had scored enough to still be in contention (in fact the judges had already decided that aggressive little McGuigan would be champion, barring a knockout). The rounds McGuigan had won he had won well. But Pedroza had sneaked a few of his own.

Now there was a vital three rounds to go, and it looked like McGuigan had to do it. The occasional shimmer in Pedroza's legs betrayed how vulnerable he was. His seconds were no longer getting out of the ring fast enough. "Seconds Out."

Thirteen . . .

The thirteenth was a time for watching the respective legs. Pedroza's were wobbly. McGuigan's were full of energy. Pedroza was doing the only thing he could, staying calm, cool, composed and patient. His composure saved him as McGuigan opened up on the third great chase of the fight.

Until then McGuigan's left was looking flat. It appeared that the fight might go the distance. The suggestion would have sent shivers down Irish spines just a couple of hours earlier. Not any more.

This was the longest and scrappiest chase — fifty seconds worth. A right did the damage, three lefts were effectively smothered then another, one that seemed certain to knock Pedroza, found the target. He stayed up.

There was a little grappling, McGuigan escaped from the clutching giant, and ran back at Pedroza like a bull letting fly a left and a right. Pedroza fell away. McGuigan tried another right. Then came more grappling and the referee had to force them apart. After another two ineffective McGuigan lefts, Pedroza ducked out of the way, then came three lefts, two of which scored. Pedroza bobbed, grappled and squared up, ducked the left again and closed McGuigan down. Again the referee called for a break. Again Pedroza opened his arms to hug McGuigan who had come at him with another bull-impression. McGuigan's might right did not pay off, and when Pedroza had seen enough daylight to throw a right of his own the round was over.

Fourteen...

Pedroza stayed cool. Pedroza stayed calm. It suited Pedroza to go down in the 14th, pushed down by McGuigan who was reprimanded for having done so. McGuigan's elbows, strapped in so tight for much of the fight, were now beginning to wander out again. But those tell-tale vibrations in Pedroza's legs showed that the fight was nearly over.

Fifteen...

Pedroza stayed cool. Pedroza stayed calm. Throughout the 15th he looked for the heavy punch only a very experienced fighter could manage in his state of wear. He also believed that he could swing a points decision. Nobody else in the stadium agreed. Cham-pee-on, Cham-pee-on, they chanted. There could be no doubt about the verdict. When the final bell sounded Pedroza raised his arm in victory. McGuigan, not to be outdone, was hoisted on to his manager's and trainer's shoulders.

Both boxers were dazed. The punters were happy. They had got their money's worth. At this level, knock-downs, blood, doesn't matter any more. Entertainment is what they want. Showbusiness with sweat, with aggression, with feeling, with emotion.

* * * * * * *

5. "You are a great champion..."

As for the rough stuff, it scarcely happened at all. Pedroza had been warned for punching low, for holding, for elbows and for not coming into the ring at the starting bell in time. McGuigan too had dropped punches to navel level or beyond, and had pushed his opponent down when it was clearly not to his own advantage. Del Rio had dashed into the ring at the end of the ninth to complain about McGuigan's three blows after the bell had gone. They all came in rapid-fire succession. The dirty stuff, according to McGuigan later, had been shared 50-50.

During sparring, McGuigan had had sparring partners that hit him low, shouldered him, kneed him in close, hit him with their elbows, stood on his toes. He wanted to learn how to cope with the dirtiest tactics and retaliate without losing his cool.

The referee strictly controlled the fight, and this, coupled with McGuigan's willingness to cope with anything dirty, prevented the fight getting out of hand in the manner of the Pedroza-Laporte fight.

When McGuigan did it, it was called "looking after yourself."

From midway through the fifteenth round it was obvious that there was going to be a big security problem keeping well-wishers out of the ring. The owners of Loftus Road, Queens Park Rangers football club, had insisted that their regular stewards should steward at the ground. During the fight thousands of fans came swarming up the aisles towards the ringside enclosure. They hopped over the barriers. They walked over press benches, fell over telephone wires, walked on phones (one fan asked *Sunday Express* journalist Frank Taylor if he could have a loan of the phone to tell his mother in Dublin he was okay), walked on notes, walked on fingers, walked on benches. One bench collapsed under the weight of a dozen fans. Some got into the ring and tried to mob the boxer. The result had not been announced by anyone except the fans. Cham-pee-on, Cham-pee-on, three staccato cries rose into the London night air again and again and again.

McGuigan and Pedroza embraced. "You are a great champion," McGuigan said. "I'm glad I didn't fight you a year ago."

Clear the ring? "Ladies and gentlemen the result will not

be announced until the ring is cleared . . . until the ring is cleared . . . until the ring is . . . ."

The American television people had already collected the scorecards from the judges and referee — "come on you guys, we've only got three minutes of air-time left."

There was no chance of clearing the ring, so they announced the result anyway . . . "Ladies and gentlemen, this is the result." Pause. "By unanimous decision." Cheers. "Barry McGuigan is the new featherweight world champee-onnnnnggggg."

Amid the roars of delight McGuigan was hugged by twenty-five year-old brother Dermot, by manager Eastwood, by trainer Shaw, by father Pat, by nine year-old brother Daniel, two year-old son Blaine, tearful wife Sandra . . . and mugged by television interviewers.

"I'd like to thank my family, in particular Mr Eastwood here who has taken me from the word go, to him thanks again. And I'm absolutely delighted. Oh good God, I'm so pleased. And you know he has treated me so well. He has spent a fortune in bringing me here. Maybe I'll repay him sometime. I'm so delighted to have beaten such a renowned champion so well.

"I'd like to take this opportunity to say one thing, I've been thinking about it all week, and I said if I won this world title I would dedicate it to the young lad that died after he fought me in 1982. I said at the start that I would like it to be not just an ordinary fighter that beat him but the World champion."

With that announcement on British and Irish television, Barry McGuigan burst into tears.

When McGuigan became champion he was one of only two white champions then recognised.

CHAPTER 2

Champion Number 22

"It's about getting bums on seats. Boxing is showbusiness, showbusiness with blood."

— Paddy Byrne, match-maker throughout Barry McGuigan's career, and cut-man in McGuigan's corner.

1. The Stuff of Legends

"If you think I'm high on Barry McGuigan, you're right." Ferdie Pacheco was medical advisor to Muhammad Ali for fifteen years. As advisor to NBC network television for seven more, he was one of the most powerful men in boxing. For him, being high is part of the boxing game.

But even by Pacheco-high standards, boxing people like himself are high on Barry McGuigan.

McGuigan was already a national hero in Ireland by the time he won the World featherweight championship in June 1985. Pacheco wants to have another legendary figure, a figure that will transcend boxing and save its image, like Muhammad Ali. He worked with Ali. He understands the qualities of living legends. He thinks Barry McGuigan will be boxing's next.

"The guy has everything. All he has to do is stay five years. He is colourful, aggressive, he boxes like a dream, he is young, handsome. He comes from a settled and close family. He has a lovely wife and child. He does his best to solve the problems of his country . . . I can't think of anything one could add to that to make him more acceptable to the public."

And with bewildering enthusiasm, *Ring* magazine, the bible of boxing, ran a cover story on the Irish champion of the world in September 1985 asking: "Can he be boxing's saviour?" They quoted Pacheco at length.

Bewildering — because Barry McGuigan was just twenty-four. He had just become one of forty or so world champions in a divided sport. He had won a disputed featherweight title, that nominated by the World Boxing Association. He had done it before what was actually a home-town crowd, dislodged and moved across the Irish Sea to London. And although he had beaten one of the greatest of the world featherweight champions, the man he dethroned, Eusebio Pedroza, was aged somewhere between twenty-nine and thirty-two and probably in a decline.

Of course McGuigan is not the only one who could save boxing in the 1980s. He just has the best chance.

And when Ferdie Pacheco identifies with a boxer, it is a good sign.

Boxing, an unashamedly mercenary and bloody sport judges success in terms of a dollar count. Make an allowance for inflation, and you get the greatest boxers of all time.

Which brings McGuigan hope in times of chaos — the chaos that followed his winning one version of the championship of the world. Chaos that puts his settled background, his close family, his image as a non-sectarian ambassador for his country, and his colourful personality, under more pressure than many of his peers can handle.

McGuigan would not take drugs. He does not drink. Does not smoke. Everywhere he goes his attractive wife Sandra is at his side. At press conferences he babbles like an auctioneer, with wit and irreverence for the world's media: "I used my entire repertoire tonight, are you sure you can spell that?" He is a real live hero. And heroes are nice, upright lads.

Heroes are also white. America, in the dusk of a white age, still likes its boxers to be white. Gerry Cooney, of doubtful ability, made ten million dollars from an interracial scrap against Larry Holmes. Ray "Boom Boom"

Mancini was hyped into the millionaire class because he was white.

McGuigan is white and Ferdie Pacheco believes that he is potentially a bigger property than Marvin Hagler or Camacho or any of them. Just as he is at his most enthusiastic, the buyer-doctor throws a curve: "funny things happen on the way to the championship."

* * * * * * *

2. Ups and Downs

Funny things had indeed happened. Every triumph in McGuigan's life was tinged with tragedy.

On the night he won the World title, the family home in Clones, ninety miles from Dublin, miles from Belfast, two hundred yards from the border that has divided Ireland since 1922, was destroyed by fire. Locals blamed the presence of television crews who had come to focus on the sight of McGuigan's mother Katie, distraught with fear and emotion, waiting in her grocery shop for the result of a fight she could not bear to watch. The lighting overloaded the out-of-date wiring system in the house.

The triumph and tragedy link almost ended his career before it was fully launched. Just as he was set for the big time, one of his opponents died as a result of injuries suffered in the ring. Asymin Muhammad, Young Ali, went into a coma after the June 1982 fight and died six months later. It almost forced McGuigan to retire.

As an amateur, he had other difficulties. McGuigan failed to dominate his weight class in Irish amateur boxing. In 1979 he was victim of a doubtful decision in the European Junior championship against a Soviet boxer. He almost did not make it to the 1980 Olympics, firstly because he could not box in the National championship final and then because the Irish Amateur Boxing Association threatened to join a United States led boycott of the Moscow Games. When he did get there, after being hyped as Ireland's top boxing medal prospect, he was beaten by a totally unknown Zambian.

And even when he turned professional and all seemed to be going well after a few fights, he was beaten by another unknown, a Brighton boxer called Peter Eubanks. That cost him his unbeaten professional record. In professional boxing, statistics count for a lot and "unbeaten" is everything.

It was not all bad. Fortunately McGuigan met the right man to further his career. Millionaire bookmaker Barney Eastwood took the amateur boxer under his wing.

Eastwood engaged the right sparring partners to improve his new boxer's technique. He even flew them in from abroad. When things started going wrong early in 1984 after an unnervingly troublesome win over Charm Chiteule he flew a coach over from New York.

Eastwood secured the match-makers who would ensure that McGuigan could beat each opponent he was given. He would thereby climb the ladder, gaining experience and looking more impressive each time.

Eastwood marketed McGuigan sufficiently well to have first the Irish, then the British, and finally the American media excited about his nice-guy, easy-talking, peace-making image. McGuigan could confide in boxing writers with breath-taking trust and confidence.

When a photographer wanted McGuigan to run through the hills, he would do so. When a television crew wanted McGuigan to sit behind the wheel of a car and drive along to the music of a song written in his honour he would do so. And when the sporting press, traditionally a confused breed as to whether they should be enthusiasts or critics of their discipline, got excited about McGuigan, the rest would be history.

With Eastwood, McGuigan got the breaks. The bookmaker ploughed over a million dollars into a bidding match against the reigning champion, Pedroza, who until then had not considered the Irishman either a serious or a lucrative contender for a World championship. Eastwood ensured that McGuigan fought for the British, and European titles, and had all of his important preliminary fights in Belfast. He ensured that McGuigan had his biggest fight in nearby London.

McGuigan contributed a lot to his own marketability and in a sense, made his own luck. His personality was one factor. His background was another.

McGuigan comes from a large Irish Catholic family. His father was a showband singer, understood charisma and publicity. He was also a boxing enthusiast who dreamed about his son becoming World champion some day.

His mother is a practical, down-to-earth Irishwoman who adores her son but never let his success go to his head. She is, as is traditional in Ireland, at the head of her family, keeping the unit close, keeping it strong, and keeping it aloof from the many pressures that accompany McGuigan's boxing career.

McGuigan himself was always fiercely dedicated. Whatever he turned his mind to, he did thoroughly and well. At the age of twelve, he turned his mind to boxing. Nowadays his knuckles are still scarred and raw as they have been throughout his career because of over-enthusiastic attacks on a punch bag. His shoulders are broad and his physical presence is such that it commands any room he enters. He might just sit down and read or watch television. Even then he seems to charge the atmosphere around him.

McGuigan is ruthless and aggressive. His fierce temper is accepted as a fact of life by those close to him. When something stands between him and what he wants, he strikes a fury that the Irish have always understood.

But then he is also gentle and loving. He loves and inspires love. In the spasmodic white heat of Loftus Road Stadium, West London, on June 8 1985, he inspired bursts of love in the hearts of millions of his countrymen.

Love for McGuigan. Love for the gentle one who could call up aggression at the flick of a button. Love for success.

* * * * * * *

3. Might Have Beens

Other funny things could have happened on the way to the

championship, but did not.

McGuigan avoided the temptation to move away from home. When he was turning professional he was attracted by offers from English managers. Instead he decided to go to Belfast, to a man whose record and reputation was unproven.

He stayed at home, stayed close to his family. He married young. Barry McGuigan was a solid family man before the affairs of the world and the poking TV cameras insinuated their way into his private life.

He survived his penchant for fast cars. Like most young, active, quick-reflex boxers, McGuigan likes to drive fast. Irish police have had a chase or two after the young tearaway. He also turned his first car upside down on one drive. And after becoming World champion when he was presented with a new Lotus, registration number BOX IT, he brought his mammy for a drive. He scratched the car.

In the earliest professional days, a largely Catholic boxing audience crowded into the Belfast hall. But boxing enthusiasts tend to come from both sides of Belfast's geographical and politico-religious divide. There were Protestant enthusiasts there too.

When he was just seventeen, McGuigan, from South of the Border (the Republic of Ireland left the British Commonwealth in 1932) was selected to represent Northern Ireland in the Commonwealth Games. The Ulster provincial branch of the Irish Amateur Boxing Association has previously selected boxers from the nine counties of Ulster, rather than just the six that remain in the United Kingdom. McGuigan's father was from Tyrone in the six counties. McGuigan disregarded the political implications of the situation and decided to go. He won a gold medal. He won it for himself.

Commonwealth champion McGuigan had to make a decision when the time came to turn professional. There are no Irish professional boxers in most weight categories, and being Irish champion carried no international prestige. Faced with this dilemma, previous Irish boxers, some of them avowed nationalists, some of them from south of the border, have fought for and won British titles.

McGuigan took out British citizenship and now holds a British passport. The citizenship was to become a contentious issue. In fact McGuigan discovered afterwards that he did not need it, he could have fought for a British title anyway.

When he won the British featherweight title, he caused immediate confusion in the international rankings charts. Some bodies accredited him as Barry McGuigan of Ireland, others as Barry McGuigan of Britain. But always, when asked who he fought for, Pat McGuigan replied, "himself."

* * * * * * *

4. New York And The Future

After winning the World championship, McGuigan was not exactly a household name in New York. The United States (New York, and even more so Atlantic City and Las Vegas), is where the boxing money is to be made.

Promoter Bob Arum and CBS boxing director Mort Sharnik watched the McGuigan-Pedroza fight together. Afterwards they went to an Irish bar in Manhattan and asked some of the people there if they had been watching the fight. Although many of them were Irish, they had never heard of Barry McGuigan.

When ABC network were advertising the fact that they had an afternoon World featherweight title fight on their schedule, they hyped up the reigning champion, Eusebio Pedroza, nineteen times a successful defender, not the challenger. The challenger was Irish. He was white. He was of major ethnic significance. He was fighting on what was practically home ground. But ABC played up Pedroza's record and reputation.

The viewership figures for the fight were disappointing. ABC recorded a rating of 5.4, which they convert to thirteen million viewers. They wanted more, but blame local baseball and the Belmont Stakes Horse Race on the rival channels for costing them viewers.

New World champion Barry McGuigan was familiar to

boxing fans only. But nobody was deterred by the fact he was still relatively unknown. Each promoter latched on to the fact he was Irish.

Heroes need to be identified with. McGuigan was white. White America could identify with McGuigan in the same way as blacks all over the world identified with Muhammad Ali.

"McGuigan could save boxing in New York," John Condon of Madison Square Garden says.

Ferdie Pacheco, doctor, television buyer, artist and friend of McGuigan (some of whose paintings were presented to McGuigan but lost in the fire at the Clones family home), agrees: "He's not quite there. But of the major new names he is at the head of the line. He is the one I would pick to be a big name.

"I think he would be somewhere between Ali and Sugar Ray Leonard. Sugar Ray had just gotten there when he had to retire with an eye injury. Ali stayed fifteen years. If McGuigan can stay for five years he can be bigger than Sugar Ray Leonard.

"I could not think of anything that could be added to his character that would make him more marketable. It all depends on the man himself, on his family, on his friends, on how they all respond to the pressure, whether he can be a top rank name or not.

"The way he stands at present, sure it is a cinch. He can be the top fighter. There are no heavyweights around. Spinks will disappear. Hagler has only another two years left. The others are messing in drugs or something like that. McGuigan is someone young kids can really look up to. And he is an exciting fighter."

Alex Wallec of ABC reckons that McGuigan is the most exciting fighter to emerge in the lighter divisions (from lightweight down) in recent years. It remains to be seen if he can match the record of Salvador Sanchez, or even Pedroza. And potentially McGuigan is more marketable than these.

The marketing has yet to be done. In early McGuigan fights televised in America, the broadcasting channels each showed a three-minute feature to introduce the Belfast boxer. They explained why they had bothered to show him at all. They showed him at home with his wife and child in Clones, they showed him with Catholics and Protestants in divided Belfast, and then they showed him entering the London ring in the most earsplitting atmosphere experienced in boxing since Muhammad Ali's time.

That was to encourage boxing fans to watch it. Boxing fans have to be intelligent to follow the politics of their sport. Four different bodies (not to mention cable television networks and publications) nominate their own champions and things tend to be confusing. Marvin Hagler maintains that even champions cannot follow who is top in what division according to what body. McGuigan became another champion, number twenty-two in descending order of weight starting from heavyweight. What caused boxing fans to latch on to this latest combination in the rubik's cube of professional boxing was the man he beat.

* * * * * * *

5. The Champ

Eusebio Pedroza arrived in New York three weeks before the twentieth defence of his WBA featherweight boxing title. He wanted to work off the last of his excess weight.

He arrived at Gleasons Gym in Manhattan, within a cheer of Madison Square Gardens, worked out briskly, sparred with Vinnie Costello and Rick Young, two of the Gym's top featherweights, and gave small clues about how he regarded this Irish challenger.

Pedroza did not seem to be serious. He was confident of wearing out the younger opponent. He even brought his wife to New York. Vinnie Costello maintains that that was a fatal move.

In boxing, sex before a fight takes everything out of the fighter. It is definitely taboo in the fight game, although not in many other sports. "And with your wife there," Costello says, "you would be inclined to mess around with her."

Young could see that Pedroza was gambling on slowing down the pace of the fight, and would be vulnerable to a hard right.

"They didn't really believe Barry was that good," Young says. "They weren't prepared for him. They thought it was just another fight. They didn't realise that Barry was as tough as he was.

"From the things they were saying about the fight I knew that.

"They thought Barry was the kind of guy who just comes straight for you and runs into punches. They didn't know he had a lot of movement, they thought he caught punches."

Pedroza barely studied McGuigan before the fight. He had coped with young tearaways before. He expected to again. He brought one sparring partner from Panama to New York with him and sliced pounds off his weight. He sparred against Young and Vinnie Costello, ironically McGuigan's two chief sparring partners when he too spent a term in Gleason's Gym in New York in 1983. With Costello he relaxed a bit. Against Young he cut loose. Gave it everything.

Young was wary. He had heard Pedroza was a dirty fighter. But in sparring he discovered that the "dirty fighter" tag was as much a part of boxing's exaggerated hype as the positive aspects of so many American champions. He grew into a close friendship with Pedroza.

"Okay, I heard rumours about weight. He looked very big. I heard he was 140-something pounds. But they were rumours. I never saw him on the scales."

Young turned down a chance to see the fight live.

"I had boxed both these guys and they had both come across to me as nice guys. Beautiful personalities.

"I had always thought of Pedroza as a bad guy. Yet he was one of the sweetest guys I ever met.

"I felt it was a tough fight and it could go either way. I had boxed with Barry before the Caba fight and I had boxed with Pedroza. I felt that Pedroza had the edge in experience.

"Pedroza wanted me to go to London, but I didn't want

to go because I was in kind of a funny position. I had been sparring with Barry and now I was helping Pedroza. I really didn't want to go. I would have loved to have seen the fight. But I really didn't want to go. Personally, I was leaning more towards Barry. Slightly."

From New York Pedroza flew to London. Young stayed in New York. When the night of the fight came around he locked himself into his living room in Harlem, switched on the television. He was going to watch his two boxers in action. He was not going to miss a punch of the action.

* * * * * * *

6. Old Score

Gerald Hayes too knew a lot about Pedroza. He felt he had got a raw deal when he fought Pedroza in Panama and the fight was stopped in the last round. The whole scene in Panama was a mess. Hayes was forced to travel to the city earlier than he intended, he had a bad flight and found he was not in peak condition when the fight came round.

Hayes was a featherweight who had become a free agent. He wanted to run his own affairs. It was difficult in the world of big-time management in America. But Hayes hung on until he got his title fight in Panama, and then had an attempt at a rematch against Bernard Taylor. Taylor won. Hayes was in decline.

"The cards were stacked against me. I was there to be an opponent, I wasn't there to win, man. They weren't going to have their man beaten. I could have beaten him if the conditions were right, but in the conditions I could not do it."

Through McGuigan, Hayes was to get a chance to wreak revenge on the Panamanian.

So Hayes arrived in Belfast three weeks before the big fight. For five to six weeks previously he had advised Barney Eastwood by phone. He knew that Pedroza was vulnerable to a right punch. If he was distracted with a left jab or a feigned punch, the right could come whizzing over the top and Pedroza could be knocked.

He came to Belfast on condition that he was a technical advisor, not a sparring partner. His purpose was to coach McGuigan's punching technique specifically with Pedroza in mind, and to show him that right punch. "I'm going to be a fighter, not a punching bag.

"I helped him long distance. You don't come with half your equipment. You come with the whole lot. I gave him everything I knew, then I came over and showed him."

Others, besides Hayes, had sensed that the vulnerability to the right punch was Pedroza's major flaw. Hayes had noticed it long before he was a championship contender entitled to fight against Pedroza. He wanted to use it to floor Pedroza when he had a crack at the title himself. But Pedroza, although he was knocked in the third round, never presented Hayes with the opportunity to do anything significant.

Hayes was approached by a boxing agent who was friendly with Eastwood, Mickey Duff, to be sparring partner for McGuigan in 1983. He enjoyed Belfast, he liked the life there and was impressed with McGuigan's manager Barney Eastwood. In his heart he longed for somebody of Eastwood's calibre to manage his own career, to look after the match-making, the sparring and the hype, and to wrangle with the political wizards who ran the sport for title fights.

For three weeks he showed McGuigan the simple tried and trusted formula — use a jab or a feint to line him up and then STRIKE.

Hayes maintains that Pedroza had probably hidden a flaw that was always there. He knew enough to cover it up and when he was a younger man, not to give anyone the opportunity to exploit it.

As it happened, the flaw probably suited McGuigan's own flaw of bringing his right too high. The punch that was to defeat Pedroza dive-bombed over a dropping defensive guard in the seventh round, Pedroza was caught with another left hook as he dropped to the ground. And never recovered.

That Hayes spent three weeks with the Irish challenger meant that McGuigan was now really confident. "I have a

CHAMPION NUMBER 22

secret move to beat Pedroza," he told the press four days before the fight. The press said "yeah" and ran the story under banner headlines. But it was important. Whether or not it would ever pay off, McGuigan could rest assured before the championship fight that he had a plan of action, that he knew something that Pedroza did not.

Country lad McGuigan likes to train near the sea.

CHAPTER 3

Into The Ring

"Anything the McGuigans did, they did it to perfection."
— Peter Duffy, Clones schoolteacher.

1. Boxing School

It was appropriate that McGuigan's thundering right should send him to World Championship victory. When he first boxed, at twelve years of age, it was that punch which distinguished him from the average juvenile boxer.

Through those early years he used the right to pulverise opponents in juvenile contests. Few of his early bouts went the distance.

McGuigan was an aggressive schoolboy. He was champion at hardy knuckles (a game like conkers, except played with bare knuckles) at school. Often ending up in scraps. Pupils would come into the headmaster with stories that McGuigan had been hitting them. Duffy remembers that McGuigan would "put manners on anyone who annoyed him." McGuigan was never vicious, just more inclined than most to end up in a scrap.

According to Duffy, McGuigan was "of good average ability in academic subjects," and possessed "an amazing combination of discipline, character, dedication and courage."

He also possessed a fearsome temper. McGuigan was not to be crossed. By the time he was in fourth class, nobody in the school would match him in a fight. His brother Dermot was in sixth class at the same time, in school. They ended up fighting each other, because there was nobody left to fight.

In 1969 a parish priest in Tannagh, near Cootehill, was dreaming up fairground attractions. He decided to set up a boxing ring, randomly select young fellows of the same age and size and match them up. One of his first and most eager customers was Barry McGuigan, then eight, revolving his hands like a windmill, and full of aggression. He beat two opponents.

Those windmill arms, prototype of the Clones Cyclone, already carried great strength. At Wattlebridge and Smithboro clubs, Barry McGuigan was soon showing the traits that would turn him into a champion, his strength and aggression.

Although strength and aggression were family traits in the McGuigans, there was no boxing in the family.

Instead they tell stories in Clones about the street-league football match that erupted into a row involving three of Barry's uncles and the grandfather, who was supposed to be an umpire.

Barry's father Pat had ambitions to be an amateur boxer but soon dropped it in favour of his singing career. Pat McGuigan became one of Ireland's best known showband singers in the days of a showband boom, the sheepskin jacket era of the 1960s. After losing his job (as did his brothers and father) when Clones Railway was closed in 1962, he travelled the roads of Ireland to sing in primitive dancehalls. He worked in England for a while. His showband career culminated in a third place in the 1967 television spectacular, the Eurovision Song Contest, with an appropriately named chanson-style ballad, 'Chance Of A Lifetime'. The proceeds of years on the road went back to setting up a small country grocery store for his wife Katie.

It was a struggle. From the struggle emerged a close family. Pat and Katie McGuigan had eight children. The two eldest boys, Dermot was born in 1960 and Barry in 1961.

Pat McGuigan fanatically followed boxing. His house was full of boxing literature. The television was always tuned to sports programmes. The two eldest sons, Dermot and Barry began to share the interest. As toddlers he brought them to local amateur promotions. Both became interested in boxing. Dermot became a spectator with an encyclopaediac knowledge of the sport. Barry became a boxer.

Although there is a strong boxing tradition in Monaghan many of the clubs formed in the county turned out to be short-lived. There was no club in Clones, and there had not been one in many years. Barry McGuigan's early boxing was with Wattlebridge club, across the border in County Fermanagh, a rural club subject to rural fluctuations.

McGuigan's mother, Kate, was worried about his crossing the border to Fermanagh in those troubled times. That, and the distance to the Wattlebridge club, resulted in Barry switching to the Smithboro club after three or four fights. Smithboro is a town eight miles from Clones on the main Monaghan Road.

The club was in its infancy. It had no clubhouse of its own and was set up in the old Smithboro schoolhouse. There was very little equipment, just plenty of young hopefuls, an enthusiastic secretary, Frank Mulligan, and an enthusiastic coach, Danny McEntee.

Though young, the club had enjoyed a brief period of success. On January 13 1974 Barry McGuigan turned up at Smithboro boxing club. He was still a few days short of his thirteenth birthday.

When Frank Mulligan, the Smithboro club secretary, was once asked what qualities he noticed in the young Barry McGuigan when he enrolled he talked about his eyes. They betrayed his fierce dedication. His fierce aggression. His fierce dedication to success in the boxing ring.

Although there was nothing distinctive about McGuigan at the start, when he was just one of a horde of youngsters sparring and boxing, his strength and his dedication were soon to mark him apart from the rest. McGuigan wanted to train all the time. He wanted to spar. He wanted to win. But where would he get sparring partners? Most of those who were the same weight (six and a half stone) in the club quickly grew wary of the Clones lad.

Danny McEntee was his coach at that stage, and described Barry McGuigan as one of the most aggressive youngsters he has ever come across. Even then he was strong. He had to be slowed down. Whereas most of the others had to work on fitness McGuigan specialised in training at home to make himself fit, and learning technique at the hall. "There's no point in me training you," McEntee told him. "I will coach you."

When a series of two-minute rounds sparring was organised, McGuigan would want three-minute rounds. He could skip for six minutes when everyone else was hard pressed to do three. At the age of fourteen he was developing a style as a go-forward boxer, taking plenty of punches to get in a few of his own.

In juvenile promotions in McCartan's Hall, McGuigan would win again and again. He always had his supporters with him, his father Pat McGuigan and brother Dermot, urging him on to victory. (This devoted encouragement pre-dated the days when Pat McGuigan would pay for petrol for cars to bring Clones people to Dublin to support his boy.) With each opponent his confidence and aggression grew. Both his father and his coach realised within months that McGuigan was good enough to succeed at national juvenile level.

The major juvenile inter-championship event was the Golden Shamrock title. McGuigan entered at thirteen, and met and beat Sean Thompson of Transport in the final. The victory drew him to the attention of the Dublin controllers of amateur boxing.

When the time came for the national under-fourteen championship, McGuigan boxed Jimmy Coughlan, then seeking a sixth juvenile title. The fight was stopped in the third round. Six-times bantamweight champion Mick Dowling was among those at the ringside that night.

In 1977, Barry McGuigan left school altogether to concentrate on boxing full-time. He had hopes of getting a job that would allow him to train and maintain a high level of fitness. Beside his name on the roll book the headmaster, Peter Duffy, entered his comment: "Unemployed Boxer".

And that was what McGuigan became. He was rejected by the army: maybe it was because he was too aggressive,

Duffy suggests.

He just worked at home around the house, in the shop, and trained. A painful amount of work to build up a level of fitness he has maintained since. Dehydrating to get his weight down to bantamweight level, seven stone seven pounds, using plastic bags, weights, exercise of every description to reach and maintain championship weight. It was tough, and the people of Clones realised his dedication and wished him sell. "Wee Barry" was going to be a boxer. There was never an alternative.

****

2. Bobbing and Weaving

Perhaps ominously, McGuigan was disqualified one night in McCartan's Hall for punching low. His only other defeat as a juvenile was in a promotion at the Transport club in Dublin.

By the age of fifteen he had begun to interpret boxing. Danny McEntee remembers that he always regarded McGuigan as a senior, and would talk to him as a senior boxer. A committee meeting of Smithboro boxing club discussed whether it was right to give McGuigan so much ring time at the expense of the other juveniles in the club. McEntee still claims that there was no favouritism granted to McGuigan. Just what he should have got. "He wanted more time, I gave him more time."

In 1977 he won the Juvenile Championships in Limerick, beat Martin Brereton in the final of the seven-and-a-half-stone division and won through his pure aggression. He won the best boxer of the night award. "He had stacks of energy, he just had to be restrained," McEntee recalls.

Brereton fancied his chances of the National title. He had just beaten Sammy McDermott, the favourite in the seven-stone seven-pounds grade in the semi-final. McGuigan should be easier. Brereton had taken up boxing at seven, McGuigan at twelve. McGuigan was a late starter in terms of top flight boxers.

But McGuigan already displayed what Brereton recalls as a vicious hook. "Like most young boxers I did not have much style then, just sheer two-fisted effort. McGuigan was already bobbing and weaving like a pro. He had an extremely professional style."

Brereton, nine times a National runner-up at various grades, later boxed at light-middleweight for Ireland. He competed in the 1980 Olympics, and counted as McGuigan's closest friend on later Irish boxing teams.

They shared a common interest. Brereton liked to fish on the canal near Edenderry. McGuigan kept ferrets in Clones, and Brereton kept falcons. A close friendship grew out of that match in Limerick.

Discussions with the Smithboro coach, Danny McEntee, at that time included use of the boxing ring to a boxer's advantage. McEntee told him that the ring was like a draught board. The old go forward, take a little punch, land a big punch style was soon to be forgotten.

A lot of work was spent trying to iron out his technical weaknesses. He tended to move to the left when he threw the left, and come too far forward. His leg stance tended to be wide and very square. His other problem was that he moved to the right when throwing a right cross. Finally, his elbows tended to stray out.

All of these were worked on in his last years as an amateur, and then tackled under Eddie Shaw as a professional. (But they still show up in times of crisis. His elbows were smartly tucked in against De Vorce, yet in the thirteenth and fourteenth rounds against Pedroza they were wandering again.)

He began to bob and weave in the ring. "Only two boxers ever at Smithboro could bob and weave naturally," Frank Mulligan recalls. "Unless you can do it naturally it cannot be taught." McEntee agrees, adding that "the tendency is for those who can do it naturally to overdo it in the ring at first."

His technique was improving in leaps and bounds. McGuigan was working on variation in his punching at this stage. His right was passing very high, like a swimmer (most noticeably in the March contest against the East

Germans in the Ulster Hall) and was inclined to go over the top. He tried to practise ways that would prevent the right going over the top. That meant using a left to the body instead of a right to the body to set up the big punch.

McGuigan found it hard working on the left hand. He did not have much faith in his left at first, but he worked on it and his natural power and dedication soon meant that this became a feared part of his armoury.

McGuigan would work for long periods on the bag, until his knuckles were raw and bleeding. He would never give them a chance to heal. He would just put a pad of cotton wool over them and get back at the bag. Soon the blood would start coming through again. "He always had skinned knuckles," McEntee recalls. "He had to be stopped on the bag. I suspect he went home and worked on the bag anyway."

He was even working on the psychology of boxing before he was eighteen. He was thinking like a pro. At night he would stand in front of the mirror trying to intimidate himself with a frozen stare. This would be reserved for the opponent in amateur contests, he almost certainly scared lads he was fighting against just by glaring at them before the first bell. He had plenty of professional videos at home. He watched them again and again, learning techniques, small insignificant-looking moves that he could try out on his amateur opponents.

He also showed no discretion whatsoever once he went into battle. McEntee would try to tell him to hold back a little during an amateur contest for a while if the opponent was not very good. He wanted McGuigan to treat some of his easier contests as sparring sessions. McGuigan was only interested in taking the opponent out as quickly and efficiently as possible.

Opponents soon learned to watch for McGuigan's low punches. "He was always a low puncher," Brereton says, "but because McGuigan is a body puncher the chances of one falling low are greater than most boxers."

He also had the capacity to land a punch after the referee called for a break, or after the bell had sounded. When the referee calls break, many boxers relax. A punch then can do more damage than several punches in the heat of the bout. It was another professional technique used by McGuigan while still in his amateur days.

McEntee taught McGuigan to minimise himself as a target. Again, as with everything he tried, he over-reacted. He moved too much, bobbed too much, a natural tendency in younger boxers. It was a case of learning to see the punch, then stop, step out of the way, back off and be ready to counter. Even at its rawest state, McGuigan's bobbing and weaving displayed considerable natural talent. For months he worked on perfecting it in Smithboro gym. Only one member of the club was left who would dare spar with him. He was the heavier Barney Maguire, a cool, disciplined, placid boxer who would take McGuigan's punches without using his greater weight against the bantamweight in moments of indiscretion.

Having decided not to limit his ring time, the next committee meeting at Smithboro that was provoked by McGuigan's exceptional talent was whether the step from juvenile to senior would be too great for the Clones man. There need have been no doubt he was senior standard.

In 1976 the Edenderry club invited over a team of boxers from England. They selected top boxers to meet them, in a promotion at the Copper Beech public house. One of the Irish prospects they selected was Phil Sutcliffe, but they had no opponent for him.

Pat McGuigan was well known in the Copper Beech as a showband singer. He was also interested in boxing. He told the organisers that his son would be able to box Sutcliffe. McGuigan was only fifteen, and Sutcliffe, later a two-time bronze medallist in the European Championships, was known as one of Ireland's finest amateur prospects. McGuigan gave a great display of body-punching and won the bout. Only a few weeks later Sutcliffe became a national senior champion.

McEntee proposed that McGuigan be entered as a senior. "It was a big step," he recalls. "If anything went wrong, I would be held responsible." In the final he met Sean Russell, nine years older than McGuigan and older brother of later British title holder Hughie Russell.

McEntee and McGuigan watched Russell in preliminary fights. They discussed his tactics, his weaknesses and the chances of beating him. It set a precedent for McGuigan's carefully planned matches in years to come. He still does not train to a pattern, rather to take on and beat boxers of individual styles.

At sixteen years of age McGuigan beat Sean Russell to become the youngest ever Ulster Senior Champion. Reporter Michael McGeary of the *Irish News* ran straight into the rapid-talking schoolboy's respectful manner — "I'd like to thank my trainer Danny McEntee and Frank Mulligan. I was only in these championships for the experience. I never dreamed . . . ."

Another fighter in the hall was coached by Eddie Shaw of the Immaculata club. Shaw eyed the new champion with interest.

The victory over Russell was just the fillip the sixteen-year-old McGuigan needed. Afterwards, Ulster Council President Eddie Thompson had a long chat with the Smithboro officials about the new champion. He wanted to know what McGuigan's connections with Northern Ireland were. They knew his grandfather was from the North, possibly his father was too. Thompson was toying with the idea of sending this polished youngster to the Commonwealth Games.

Freddie Gilroy told the *Belfast Telegraph* journalist Jack Magowan afterwards: "He is the greatest prospect I have ever seen. He punches well and hard with closed gloves." Former Gilroy opponent and one-time World Champion Johnny Caldwell said that McGuigan's hands worked with the speed of a pneumatic drill. "He has a bomb in both hands."

In March, shortly after his seventeenth birthday, McGuigan boxed against East Germany for Ulster in Belfast. His performance confirmed him as a Commonwealth Games favourite. There had been a precedent. Pat Doherty had boxed for Northern Ireland in the 1970 Commonwealth Games, winning a bronze medal, even though he was from Ballyshannon in County Donegal. Smithboro were posed with the question of whether he should go.

Another committee meeting was dedicated to McGuigan.

****

3. Medals

President of the Ulster Council of the Irish Amateur Boxing Association, Eddie Thompson, had been watching McGuigan's progress. "We knew this lad was something special. We applied to headquarters for the necessary permission in September 1977 to consider him for the Commonwealth Games." Before even the Ulster seniors, Thompson had worked out McGuigan was eligible for the games through his father.

The Ulster Council recommends boxers to the Commonwealth Games Council. They then organise collective training and since the 1958 Commonwealth Games in Cardiff they are proud of their record of five gold, five silver and fourteen bronze medals.

McGuigan was ambitious. In early 1978 he had even boxed in a test for the European Junior Championships at Drogheda against Holmes. McGuigan won with a fearsome display of body-punching but was considered too young by the IABA. He was disgusted. This time there was no holding him back. He was seventeen at the time of the Commonwealth Games in 1978. The pain and the agony of the early stages, working himself into peak fitness which he has maintained without any problem since, were all forgotten in the aftermath of those games, when he won a gold medal at Edmonton.

McGuigan's opponents in four victories (two inside the distance) were from Scotland, Guyana, Rannelli of Canada and Tumat Sagolik of Papua New Guinea ("You would want to have seen him, he had arms like JCBs," McGuigan was to comment on his return). McGuigan was lucky to get the verdict against Sagolik. But it was the last break he got in an amateur career. His biggest thrill as an amateur came in his first year at senior level.

It also set a valuable precedent — a strong dividing line

between sport and politics in the McGuigan approach. He was Irish. He had Northern Irish parentage, so he was qualified to box for both. That boxing was a 32-county sport (as are all major sports in Ireland with the exception of soccer and athletics) made it easier to meet the problems his dual nationality posed. McGuigan was winning a medal not for a province or a nation, but for himself. Smithboro gave him approval before he went out to Edmonton for the Commonwealth Games. Clones gave theirs when he returned, in the form of a civic reception.

Their next civic reception for McGuigan would celebrate his winning the World Championship.

In October 1978 Barry McGuigan went to Rotterdam for a multi-nations tournament and took another gold medal. In January 1979 he made his international debut, and featured as one of Ireland's winners in a 10-1 destruction of Scotland for the Kuttner Shield.

At first the young boxers on the Irish amateur team did not know how to handle this newcomer. He was, in the words of Hughie Russell, "a country lad.

"When we talked about girls and discos and things like that he talked about hunting." Belfast fellows on the Irish team used the term country lad even for the Dubliners. McGuigan fitted into neither category. He was a genuine country lad.

He was also incredibly serious. When he won his gold medal in Rotterdam, he would not join his colleagues for a disco. He went to bed instead, got up the next morning and trained.

He won another gold medal in a 1979 multi-nations tournament, in Rumania. But McGuigan was not to win another Irish title, missing the championships because of a cut eye sustained against Kenny Bruce in the Ulster seniors.

That cut eye cost him a second Ulster title. He was disconsolate afterwards, gashed and bloody in the dressing room, when an old boxing fan that he did not know came to console him. "Don't worry," he was told, "you have a bright future ahead of you." The man was Barney Joe Eastwood, bookmaker tycoon.

4. Disappointments

It should have been a steady rise from such a promising beginning to his amateur career. At fifteen he had beaten Sutcliffe shortly before Sutcliffe became a National Senior champion. At sixteen he was an Ulster Senior champion. At seventeen he was a National Senior champion and Commonwealth Games gold medallist. Shortly before his eighteenth birthday he made his international debut for Ireland. But things were to go wrong for the last two years of his amateur boxing. For instance, he only won one National Senior championship in three years.

This period was to be characterised by frustration, injury, controversy and disappointment.

First, there was what should have been an easy capture of the National Junior championship. After all, McGuigan was already Ulster Senior champion. Instead, he lost the final to Michael Holmes of Phoenix club.

Holmes was an easygoing character, and still claims that he never had the sort of dedication McGuigan had when it came to boxing. He liked his pint between training sessions, and was rarely one hundred per cent fit. But he showed considerable prowess in the ring and was not intimidated by McGuigan's reputation.

"The name affected a lot of Barry McGuigan's opponents. Names mean nothing once that bell goes."

Holmes fought McGuigan three times in 1978. The second bout was a match-off for the European Junior Championships. It took place in the Rossnaree Hotel in Drogheda and McGuigan won with a great display of body-punching. But he was angry to discover that he was two months under-age (the age limit was seventeen to nineteen) afterwards. He felt the IABA should have informed him of this even before the contest.

Holmes was selected for the European Championship, and while McGuigan went on to pick up a Commonwealth Games gold Holmes won a silver medal at the European Championship.

Both boxers made the step to senior level in the same year, 1978. Both were still extremely young, seventeen in both cases, when they met at the National Bantamweight final in April 1978. This time McGuigan won, again by a close decision.

Holmes was selected for several boxing internationals afterwards, including the American tour when he was stopped by future world title contender Bernard Taylor. When he was due to meet McGuigan again in the 1980 National Senior final he was stripped off in the dressing room waiting for his call when the news came through that McGuigan had withdrawn with an injured hand. Later he heard that McGuigan had been selected for the Olympics, although Holmes felt he should have at least a match-off as he was national champion.

The Holmes -v- McGuigan selection argument was probably based on the fact that McGuigan had performed better in international competition. Holmes packed in boxing for a period. When he returned to amateur boxing with Arbour Hill a broken hand ended his career and lost him his job.

"Boxing is a poor man's sport. McGuigan had some advantages over the rest of us when it came to backing. When he broke his hand in 1980, he was sent to London by his father for specialist treatment. When I broke my hand, I was sent to Jervis Street."

McGuigan damaged that hand in the semi-final stage of the 1980 Irish Championship against Damien Fryers and missed another Irish title. Yet he was automatic bantamweight selection for the Olympic Games.

McGuigan's temper was to cost him dear. When he was told to rebandage his hand against Richie Foster in Dublin before one bout at the National Stadium, he threw off the bandages in a rage and slipped on his gloves without any protection.

After the fight against Foster he found he had knocked out the *meta carpel* in his left hand and dislocated a knuckle and fractured a support bone in his right. The hand injury still affects the amount of time he spends at the punchbag.

But it was not injury that made his amateur career miserable. It was three costly decisions, all of them on points, all of them bouts that McGuigan feels strongly that he should have won.

They came against Soviet Union boxer Juri Gladychev in the European Junior Championships at Rimini in 1979. The third was in the ABA Centenary Tournament final against Scotland's Ian McLeod in October 1980. The middle one, and most important of all, was against Zambian Wilfred Kabunda in the 1980 Olympics.

Despite hand trouble, McGuigan was selected for the May 1979 European Junior championships in Rimini. Seven Irish boxers were selected — Garry Hawkins, Dave McAuley, Richie Foster, McGuigan, David Irving and Martin Brereton.

It was a painful introduction to the suspect judging of European amateur boxing.

McGuigan beat Dragon Kohovalov of Yugoslavia to reach the semi-finals and meet Soviet boxer Juri Gladychev. McGuigan punched magnificently against Gladychev but was beaten on points according to the judges.

France's judge Buonovista made it 59-55 to Gladychev, Roelands of Belgium made it 59-58 and Angelov of Bulgaria 59-58. The Italian judge Tallerico voted for McGuigan 59-58, and Jensen of Denmark 60-57.

Felix Jones of the Irish Amateur Boxing Association protested. The seven jury members agreed that McGuigan should have won. McGuigan threatened to retire in anger after the verdict.

The 1980 Olympics were the high point of a crowded boxing year that saw internationals against Scotland, England, Hungary, West and East Germany.

Irish interest in the Olympics was fixed on four or five medal prospects: athletes John Treacy and Eamonn Coghlan, Flying Dutchman sailors David Wilkie and Jamie Wilkinson, and boxers Barry McGuigan and Terry Christle.

But in May the news broke of the American boycott of the Olympics, as a gesture of protest against the invasion of Afghanistan. Several countries followed suit. The Olympic Council of Ireland left the final decision on whether to go or not to its affiliated sports federations. The first two to withdraw were the equestrian team, which needed government finance to transport horses to the Soviet

Union, and the boxers.

The Irish Amateur Boxing Association has strong ties with the United States, had recently been on tour there, and were well aware that there would be an "alternative Olympics" tournament for boxers of a high standard from boycotting nations.

But a wave of protest swept through the clubs, the decision was reversed, and McGuigan had his medal chance.

As the government had decided not to sanction any grant-aid to the Olympic Council of Ireland, a massive fund-raising effort got under way. In the end a full Irish team travelled.

The IABA organised a training camp in Drogheda in preparation for the games under coach Gerry Storey. McGuigan brought his cassette recorder and music for diversion and settled into a last bout of severe training.

Collective training was a new development in Irish Olympic preparations. It had been organised for previous Commonwealth Games, including Edmonton. It had been introduced for Irish Olympic teams in 1976.

In 1980 the IABA used the Rossnaree Hotel, outside Drogheda about forty miles from Dublin and sixty miles from Belfast. The hotel management facilitated them by installing showers and gym facilities. The boxers were brought out for exercise on the beach in the morning.

McGuigan was brought to the session by his enthusiastic father. Among the visitors to the camp was his girlfriend, Sandra, the woman he was to marry in eighteen months time. The authorities took a dim view of boxers' girlfriends appearing on the scene. "Oh McGuigan," Eddy Thompson throws his eyes to heaven when he thinks back. She was the only person who ever came between McGuigan and his boxing ambition.

It had been a long season, continuous boxing and training through the 1978-'79 season after the Commonwealth Games, the 1979 European Championship in May, and the hectic and early starting 1979-'80 season in preparation for the Olympics. He was beginning to feel the pressure of the prolonged season. Colleague Martin Brereton actually decided to pull out of the team and went home for a week-end before being persuaded to return. Terry Christle was unceremoniously dropped from the selection when he failed to show up at all, preferring to train under former Olympic silver medallist Fred Teidt in Dublin. With Christle gone, the pressure was on McGuigan to win a gold medal.

McGuigan won his first contest at the Olympics in devastating style. He forced Issack Mabushi of Tanzania to take three counts in the third round of his first round match.

McGuigan had been cautioned twice for slapping as he tried to put his opponent away in the third round. Otherwise it was a happy, true-to-plan affair, McGuigan even thought he won the first round: "I was testing him out" — while the rest of the Irish camp were worried by his typical slowness to start. Some of the judges gave the first round to Mabushi. A bad omen.

Maybe it was because McGuigan's rights were straying a little too high. Gerry Storey, the Irish coach, told him to keep them down a bit. "Aim for the chest," he was told. But Storey and manager Eddie Thompson were also convinced McGuigan was ahead after the first round.

Not that it mattered. After thirty seconds of the last round McGuigan delivered what was described as the "punch of the night", a right to Mabushi's jaw, and forced a count. The fight was eventually stopped with thirty seconds to go.

The Moscow crowd jumped to their feet, cheering and clapping.

An argument developed between the Irish handlers and the Olympic officials. They wanted Ireland's doctor, Moira O'Brien to accompany McGuigan to the dope test. The Olympic officials eventually conceded the point.

As McGuigan left the ring he said to Eddy Thompson "I want to pump." But all had changed by the time he was brought to the medical centre.

McGuigan could not produce any fluid. They doused him in cold water. They gave him tea to drink. They gave him fruit juice. They told him not to be letting himself down in front of the lady doctor. But McGuigan could not produce enough fluid to have a dope test. They would not even let him go away to change. Considering that a boxer spends a lot of time before a bout dehydrating and then perspires in the ring, McGuigan's dilemma was understandable. It took three hours to get through the dope test.

Then came problems. The officials wanted to know about traces that showed up in the test. McGuigan was taking tablets for a chest infection. The situation was explained when the medicine was produced.

When he returned to the Irish camp there were few celebrations. There was a medal to be won.

The win was greeted with jubilation, especially after a series of disappointments experienced by the other boxers on the Irish squad. McGuigan, John Treacy and Eamonn Coghlan were the three big hopes for Irish medals at the 1980 Olympics. None of them got any. Instead a yachting silver and Hugh Russell's boxing bronze was Ireland's haul from the games the United States and their sphere of influence boycotted.

Wilfred Kapunda of Zambia should not have been a tough opponent, but McGuigan went out in the next round. The big right was nowhere to be seen, one little right sneaked over the top of Kapunda's guard in the second and it seemed for an instant that the Zambian might take a count, but it was not to be.

Kapunda punched consistently, if not solidly, and it was a case of volume against power at the end. So exit McGuigan. Storey, Thompson and McGuigan all cried foul about the decision.

"I thought I won the fight," McGuigan complained. "He was only flicking out his hand. I landed far more solid punches and kept pressurising him." Thompson maintained that the Cuban and Soviet judges wanted McGuigan out of the championship to protect their own boxers. Four of the judges decided Kapunda had won, those from the Soviet Union, Algeria, Cuba and Argentina. One from Jamaica gave the bout to McGuigan. All marked the fight 59-58.

The jury were evidently surprised at the decision, but there was no question of robbery such as happened in Rimini the previous year.

Afterwards there was a lot to be said about the Olympic failure. McGuigan was immensely disappointed. He felt he had let his followers down, "not just himself, but really he felt for all the people that expected him to win a medal for them," Pat McGuigan recalls. McGuigan himself pointed to the fact that he had probably over-trained, probably got too tense about it all. The fight against the Zambian had been scrappy. Kapunda was tall, awkward, and McGuigan lacked authority. Too much had been left to chance, to the Olympic judges. The great ambition of the Olympic medal was to be forgotten.

The disappointments of Rimini and Moscow were the lowest points of McGuigan's amateur career. On both occasions he threatened to retire. "There were times when I felt like giving it all up, especially after what happened in Moscow and Rimini. But then I would come back to this boxing mad house."

Nobody believed McGuigan when he had claimed, at eighteen years of age, that he would retire from boxing after the 1979 European Junior Championship. Yes, he had eventually decided, he would keep going until the Olympics.

Now, when the disappointment of the Olympics hit him, he thought about retiring again. Yet, within days of the Olympic defeat, and still in Moscow, he was talking about his next contest. He even occasionally mentioned turning professional to colleagues. From an early stage, McGuigan had talked about his chances if he turned pro.

The disappointments were not over. In Wembley in October, McGuigan lost a third split decision that he should have won, against Scotland's Ian McLeod in the Amateur Boxing Association centenary tournament. By now he was considering turning professional on a regular basis. He had already sparred with professionals, he knew the story.

The three disappointments were not, in retrospect, of major consequence. The Rimini failure was the most controversial, neutrals were less sure that he had done enough to beat Kabunda in the Olympics. The McLeod defeat was a consequence of his slow start.

McGuigan could have perfected his remaining defects in the amateur ranks. Instead, he turned professional. That way he could straighten out the defects and get paid for doing so.

McGuigan had, in his own words, gone to the top. There was nothing there for him but disappointment. There was nowhere left to go.

Partners in punch-power: The relationship between McGuigan and manager Barney Eastwood has been paternal from the start.

CHAPTER 4

The Pro Game

> *"At the end the Nigerian was thrown on the canvas and took half a minute to recover but the generous applause from the dinner-suited audience was a fine testimony to a brave boxer of whom more will be heard without a doubt."*
> — Irish Times report of the McGuigan -v- Young Ali fight in June 1982.

1. Young Man In A Hurry

McGuigan left amateur boxing with a great sense of disappointment in the Irish Amateur Boxing Association. Small things had annoyed him, like their nominating him to fight Ian Clyde in Canada and asking him to pay most of his own fare. Asking too much of youngsters who were by and large, working class, perpetually short of money, and unemployed.

McGuigan conceded in his first few months as a professional that he would have stuck it out as an amateur if he could have got a job. The thought hardly bears examination now that he is champion of the world.

IABA vice-president Johnny Connors, since deceased, from Drogheda, even went to some trouble to find McGuigan a job. It did not work out.

Eddie Thompson had tried to get McGuigan nominated for a scholarship to the United States in 1978. This would have given his amateur career a major boost, pushing him into the right coaching environment just as he had achieved his first major success at the Commonwealth Games in Edmonton. That fell through, probably because McGuigan had left school after his Intermediate Certificate examination at sixteen years of age and had no real academic qualifications. Other sportsmen, incidentally, have managed to survive without Irish qualifications in America (an example is golfer Philip Walton who went to America, loved the golf, hated the study, the same reason why he never bothered to sit the Leaving Cert.)

Instead when McGuigan was seventeen and full of potential, he began to get disenchanted with the amateur boxing set-up and was deprived of his first coach, Danny McEntee, who left Smithboro after a disagreement with Frank Mulligan. There followed the series of three morale-crushing disappointments at Rimini, Moscow and the ABA Centenary tournament at Wembley.

McGuigan would have liked a job that would have given him ample time to train and perfect his boxing skills. With the right job, he felt he could progress to even greater heights in amateur boxing.

He was wary of turning professional. The big attraction about turning professional was money — the legendary amounts that top boxers could earn. But the amount of money that could be made depended very much on the length of the career. He felt that an average professional boxer might have to spend over ten years in paid fighting to make money. That was too long in McGuigan's timescale.

That timescale was to profoundly affect his career. He was a young man in a hurry. He wanted, not just to get to the top, but to get there very quickly. He wanted not just to make money, but to do it quickly. This rush, rush, hurry, hurry philosophy was instrumental in turning the disappointed Smithboro amateur into the Clones Cyclone, Champion of the World.

He was being constantly advised by boxing observers about how slow he was to feel his way into a fight, how often he put himself at a thirty-three per cent disadvantage by losing the first round, and how good a professional he would be.

They included the professional managers in whose gyms McGuigan had sparred. Lawless in Glasgow, after watching McGuigan sparring with Jim Watt was impressed with the youngster. "An Irish amateur, McGuigan is his name," he was told. He noted it and made an approach.

The big name of English boxing promotion for the past ten years, Mickey Duff, really Maurice Praeger, the Hungarian with the Irish sounding alias, made an approach to McGuigan. In my case, he said, I don't normally approach boxers. Usually *they* come to *me*. Duff left McGuigan with an offer of an open plane ticket for himself and his father to fly to London and test the set-up. Duff deals in world champions and potential world champions. He had the know-how and the contacts. He is used to picking winners.

There were others — names from the British boxing manual of managers, Eddie Thomas, Peter Keenan, Derry Treanor, all experts in the constant scouting for talent that continued at every major amateur promotion and championship.

McGuigan had two priorities in choosing a manager. One was that he could trust him. The other is that he could stay at home, as close to home as possible.

One vital approach came from Barney Eastwood to Pat McGuigan during a contest at the Ulster Hall. McGuigan was fighting Damien Fryers, later to become an Eastwood professional boxer himself, in the ring. At the ringside Eastwood, whom McGuigan knew by sight but had never spoken to, suggested to Pat McGuigan that the three three-minute rounds of amateur boxing were too short for McGuigan.

In his opinion, McGuigan should be doing the three rounds in the dressing room and then coming out and doing ten more. He thought McGuigan would make a good professional. "As a matter of fact," Pat McGuigan replied, "he's been thinking along the same lines himself."

Eastwood said to give him a telephone call if he was interested. Months later, Pat McGuigan was to think of Eastwood and dig out the phone number. Before his son decided to go ahead and take up Mickey Duff's offer of the trial period in London. The man whom McGuigan had seen regularly at boxing matches with Gerry Storey. The man who had consoled McGuigan after his cut eye against Kenny Bruce in the Ulster Hall.

By then some basic family arguments had been sorted out. Barry's mother, Katie McGuigan, is a placid woman, who prizes friends and abhors violence. The sort of woman one would expect to dislike the caged violence of the boxing ring.

She was worried about Barry as an amateur. She did not like him boxing. Fame could hardly compensate for her distrust of the sport.

Her husband Pat was a boxing fan. He wanted his sons to achieve some of the great heights he had thought about himself as a boxer before he went into a showband career. Barry's turning professional excited him.

And there the two differed. They fought it out again and again. Katie said no. Pat said yes. They decided to leave the decision to Barry anyway. The father and son had their way. Pat will recall, half-in-earnest, that he nearly had to move out of the house when the decision was being made.

Coping with that moral crisis was a good start for Barry McGuigan. Few boxers have had to cope with the morality of the sport of boxing as dramatically as he had afterwards.

And when the decision was made, and a boxer died of injuries he sustained fighting McGuigan in a professional bout, Katie McGuigan never once said "I told you so."

* * * * * * *

2. Barney Eastwood

McGuigan went to stay with the Eastwood family for ten days. There he was treated very well, and according to agreement the relationship turned out to be paternal from the start.

In ancient Celtic Druidic lore, the seventh son has all manner of mystical powers.

Barney Joe Eastwood had six sons. He told McGuigan

that he would become the seventh son.

Most of McGuigan's suspicions, aroused by stories of other Irish boxers being cheated by dodgy managers across channel, were quickly forgotten.

Eastwood was a very wealthy man. He had already made his money. Why would he need to cheat McGuigan? Eastwood was in management because of his love of boxing.

Barry's father, Pat, warned his son about his previous experiences with dancehall promoters.

McGuigan decided that the Eastwood opportunity could not be turned down. It offered him what he wanted most, a chance to take on the world from his own home in Clones.

Barney Eastwood was born in 1932 in Cookstown, County Tyrone. The family had a hardware shop in the town. Eastwood left school at fourteen to make his way into the hard business world of late 1940's Northern Ireland.

The Eastwood family were soon prominent in Cookstown business life. One cousin now runs a chain of twelve shoe shops throughout Northern Ireland. Another has a massive scrap business. B.J. Eastwood bought a pub in Carrickfergus and started taking bets there. Soon he was a bookmaker. Now his bookmaking empire has thirty-two branches throughout Northern Ireland.

His involvement with sport began in Gaelic football, and he played for the Tyrone under-18 team that won the All-Ireland final at Croke Park. He was banned for playing soccer. He has since retained an interest in, but little respect for the GAA.

He became interested in boxing when he watched American soldiers slugging it out at a base near his Cookstown home. He became involved in promotion briefly at the tail-end of the 1950's boxing boom in Belfast, the days of Gilroy and Caldwell, and soon ran into trouble with the British Boxing Board of Control.

After that he packed it in, but saved the experience for another day.

His bookmaking empire is based in Castle Street, now an ecumenical corner of what was formerly a Catholic business area with multinationals and travel agencies congregated into the edge of the Belfast city centre control zone. There he set up a gym for McGuigan to train in.

His six sons all work on aspects of the Eastwood empire. Stephen promoted the world title fight, for which his father would provide the star boxers. Brian became McGuigan's publicity agent.

And the father's empire goes rolling on. Shortly after he met McGuigan he bought the Russell Court Hotel in Belfast for £1 million. The hotel had lain idle for ten years since it had been bombed by the IRA. He owns the Dunmurry Shopping Centre in South Belfast, the Newells building in Royal Avenue, and other properties in Berry Street (off Royal Avenue) and on the Ormeau Road. As for the hotel, he claims he has no idea what he intends to do with it.

His betting shops, according to Belfast magazine *Board Room*, employ 150 people and turn over £15 million a year.

In an era of discrimination against Catholics in Northern Ireland, Eastwood's horizons were largely defined by his religion. But he made a lot of money from the working class traits of drinking and gambling, and was eventually even able to boast of betting shops in both the Falls and the Shankhill.

Boxing was another love of the Belfast working classes. Eastwood was once quoted as saying "the whole town goes broke for two weeks before one of (McGuigan's) fights."

He also enjoyed a close friendship with most of those involved in amateur boxing in Belfast and regularly attended promotions. There he saw the opportunity of restarting professional boxing in Belfast when he came across the slow-starting, but extremely talented Barry McGuigan.

Eastwood had watched the comings and goings of world boxing in the years since his own initial forage into promotion. He realised that the key to the top was the right class of sparring partner.

His immense wealth meant that he had the capacity to fly sparring partners from all over the world to Belfast. With the right sparring partners, coupled with a well chosen set of opponents, and a shrewd marketing image, McGuigan could become a championship contender. The relationship was set up on a paternal basis. McGuigan was warned he would have to fight for buttons at the start. But he would get every assistance from the man McGuigan constantly refers to as Mr Eastwood. In the end he was to become closer to Eastwood than some of his own sons.

Eastwood had a reputation for being ruthless, ruthless in business, and then ruthless in his management of McGuigan. He made the decisions. He controlled media access to the boxer. He barred a BBC reporter from the Castle Avenue gym for asking questions about how much Eastwood's boxers earned. He barred the *Sunday Tribune* from fights for criticism of McGuigan's low punching after the Chiteule fight.

Then when *Ulster News Letter* journalists took industrial action he withdrew advertising from the newspaper in support of the journalists.

His hobbies include collecting antique French period furniture and breeding alsation dogs.

To his £300,000 mansion on the slopes of Cultra he brought McGuigan, and gave him a taste of the trappings of wealth that the fighter might some day enjoy. A Mercedes for everyday driving, a Rolls Royce for big occasions such as fight nights, Eastwood's flamboyance added an intriguing flavour to the revival of professional boxing in Belfast.

This was Eastwood's bid for fame. His picture on fight tickets. His name tagged to that of a world champion.

* * * * * * *

3. Marketing Mr Nice Guy

McGuigan's new trainer was Eddie Shaw, who had grown up in the heady days of the 1950s when Tommy Madden, Joe Anderson, Sean Hanna, Sean Wilson and the last Irish world champion Johnny Caldwell were all colleagues of Shaw's at the Immaculata club under Jack McCusker.

Shaw won his first Irish championship at four stone in 1953. He was Ulster and Irish Junior Champion. In 1961 he won the Ulster Senior title at bantamweight and turned professional under Jimmy McAree in 1962, missing a chance of going to Australia with the Northern Ireland team.

His professional career was short and unsuccessful financially. But he had a marvellous record of twelve wins in fourteen fights. A recurring injury in his right hand forced him to retire at the age of twenty-two.

He retired in September 1964 and was back in amateur boxing soon afterwards, as trainer to the Immaculata club.

He trained alongside Freddie Gilroy and Johnny Caldwell. He knew what the pro game was all about. He quickly set to work on McGuigan's new levels of fitness required and his technique.

Marketing was an important part of the Eastwood master plan. McGuigan was pleasant, courteous and witty. He always described his manager as Mr Eastwood. He was closely protected from any damaging media interest. Any questions about the Falls and the Shankhill and Divided Ulster were carefully monitored. So was the question of money. McGuigan was not to be identified as someone from the other side of the Irish border, what Unionists would call a "Free Stater". That would be suicidal in the revival effort for Belfast boxing.

There was also the question of identity: the best, most neutral identity could be assumed with the nickname of Young Barry. Tracksuits were printed with that logo: Young Barry. But Young Barry never caught on.

Although it immediately gave away his origins, south of the Irish border, the more catchy Clones Cyclone was to become the nickname.

Eastwood worked hard to keep the McGuigan dream out of any of the sticky areas of religion or politics. It was to pay off in the months after the British title when he became a fully grown peacemaker.

Most of the marketing was already inadvertently done by McGuigan. He married a very photogenic wife. He came from a large, friendly family. His background if not exactly working class, was at least small town — "country lad" stuff. The McGuigan man, the Clones Cyclone, seemed to come straight out of *Little House on the Prairie*. John Boy Walton with boxing gloves.

The story about the sacks of spuds building up the strength in his arms, and the daddy who made money out of showbusiness and built a gym at the family home for his son were all highly homely, family-paper stuff.

The Eastwood connection introduced power and money, the paternal manager.

And the little litany after every fight, to whom the thanks are due etc etc added to it.

Eastwood was on a winner. McGuigan's Mr Nice Guy image has intrigued journalists ever since he started in professional boxing. All that was needed was the exact opposite inside the boxing ring — the aggressive fighter, complete with fangs. The Jekyll-and-Hyde effect was good for McGuigan, good for all who rode with him, and good for boxing.

* * * * * * *

4. Victories and Defeat

McGuigan had a little litany to answer any question about the differences between amateur and professional boxing when he was still fresh into the paying side of the sport: "You need to be strong, durable, to be ready to kick back when you're getting a beating, to concentrate for those twenty-four minutes, to never relax, even when he is relaxing, to think, think, think all the time, and you need every bit of experience you can get . . . it's like a 100-metre runner suddenly becoming a 1,500-metre runner."

He found he needed a different type of fitness, and found plenty of people to advise him on what type of fitness that was. He thought that by two years, maybe 1983, he would be a good pro. In fact it took him one year and eleven months to win the British title.

He wanted plenty of pressure early on. He wanted to be

able to contend for the British title within ten or twelve months of turning professional. In his third fight he was topping the bill — "It's a lot of pressure but it will help in the long run." He wanted to build up a record. To draw the crowds. To bring boxing back to Belfast. A young man in a hurry.

McGuigan's first purse was £400. He was now a full-time boxer, expecting to box an average of once a month. He went into debt to cover his living expenses. Before major fights, he lived with the Eastwoods in Cultra. The rest of the time, he lived at home with his family.

In the beginning McGuigan exposed himself too much. He was too enthusiastic to land his favourite punch as an amateur, the right uppercut to the head. He had to learn to be more cautious.

His most valuable lesson was a half-point defeat in only his third contest, over eight two-minute rounds against Peter Eubanks in August 1981. McGuigan was fortunate to survive his next eight-rounder, a one point defeat of Jean Marc Renard in September 1981. But McGuigan was learning.

He beat Luis de la Sagra over eight rounds in January 1982. The next boxer to go the distance with him was pre-World Title fight opponent Juan Laporte in February 1985.

Nobody since Renard has knocked McGuigan.

Building up a good record is important to impress promoters and publicists. McGuigan's record was built in early 1982 against little-known opponents, men he could beat, who served the purpose. He averaged under three rounds a fight for one four-month period.

Charlie Nash was the last Irishman to fight for a world title. On May 10 1981, Nash's big-time career came to an abrupt end at the hands of Joey Gibilisco, at Dalymount Park. On the same bill, Barry McGuigan made his debut against Selvin Bell in a scheduled six-rounder.

The fight was delayed until the end of the night, and McGuigan admitted to feeling racked with nerves by the prospects of this opener. Jamaican born, Manchester based, Selvin Bell was a rough looking character, but basically a "have gloves will travel" third rate boxer. A well-chosen opponent for a beginner. He lasted less than two rounds against McGuigan's body punching. McGuigan won with a right hook to the body.

The night was a promotional disaster. Only 2,000 had showed up. There were few around when McGuigan made it to the ring. Four supporters had come from Clones. Making an impact in the world of small-time professional boxing was not a priority. First boxers must build up their own confidence. Owen McCormack was the match-maker chosen by the Eastwoods to pick McGuigan's early opponents.

A month after that debut, McGuigan faced Gary Lucas of Liverpool on the undercard of another world title fight, Alexis Arguello against Jim Watt. McGuigan defeated Lucas for the first time when the referee stopped the fight in the fourth round.

There are plenty of workhorse boxers around for a young boxer to build his reputation with. Most of these will never get anywhere, they just collect their few quid and a trip to Belfast, are beaten and are happy with that. Elsewhere there are other young boxers who hope eventually to make it, and these are often worth looking up for a contest. One such boxer was Peter Eubanks, a Brighton prospect.

The Eubanks fight, on August 3 1981, was to attain a significance in retrospect.

Paddy Byrne was the promoter of the programme in Brighton. He was also becoming more and more the match-maker for Eastwood. He saw that Peter Eubanks had three wins in seven fights. He would undoubtedly offer stiff opposition to the young McGuigan. And McGuigan should be able to beat him.

So he arranged for an eight three-minute rounds fight. Just days before the fight, the British Boxing Board of Control wrote back to him to say that Eubanks was not allowed to box three-minute rounds.

The Board of Control had strict regulations for boxers who are newly turned professional. One is that they must have a recognised manager, someone who will be responsible for them for the first year. After that they can become a free agent. Then they get a licence limiting them to six or eight rounds, and in some cases of younger boxers the licence can specify two minute rounds. Byrne had never thought that this restriction applied to Eubanks. Eubanks had turned nineteen only four months earlier.

He telephoned Eastwood with the bad news. Eastwood was upset. He explained that McGuigan was a slow starter, that after two minutes he was just finding himself and that the whole point of his great potential as a professional was that nine minutes was just not enough for him. He only came into his own at the end of a round and after two or three rounds of a fight. Byrne apologised. He knew McGuigan from his amateur days and realised that two-minute rounds meant bad news.

Eastwood insisted on another opponent. Byrne said it was too late. That McGuigan should beat Eubanks anyway. That the fight should go ahead.

Overenthusiasm was blamed for McGuigan's defeat in Brighton. He chased Eubanks and ran into a few flying rights at vital moments. The Eastwood camp all felt that McGuigan had won. He had Eubanks down twice but failed to finish him. At one stage he even thought the referee was going to stop the fight and award it to McGuigan. But a slow start cost him points. Referee Ronald Dakin reckoned there was half a point in it, 78½-78.

Eubanks still works in Brighton, now more concerned that his twin brother Simon should be successful in the fight game. Afterwards he did not achieve much in boxing, but still carries the reputation as the only man to have beaten McGuigan. Four years later, he was dismissive about the result. "It was a job. You forget it. McGuigan just was not as good then."

* * * * * * *

5. Bum-a-month

The morning after the Brighton fight Paddy Byrne and

Eastwood walked along the beach with McGuigan for a where-do-we-go-from-here discussion.

It was a highly significant moment. The day McGuigan cried on Eastwood's shoulder and wondered would he ever make it.

Eastwood said some daft things to console his boxer, like telling him that he was going to be world champion some day.

They went over the fight again and agreed that the decision was a bad one, but maybe it was valuable. The pressure of an undefeated record was removed. Valuable lessons about leaving things up to the scorecard were learned. McGuigan learned about some of his inadequacies. Eastwood did too. The career was to be carefully plotted in future. A fight a month, no slip-ups. The psychological effect of this defeat was to reduce McGuigan to tears on Brighton beach. Another defeat could be worse.

Eastwood told McGuigan to prepare for a triumphant home-coming. A boxing promotion in the Ulster Hall.

The Ulster Hall, an ancient Victorian theatre, had always been renowned as a boxing venue in Belfast. By setting a ring in the middle of the hall, with the boxes and galleries leaning steeply down to gaze on the action, a promoter could guarantee a great view from the cheapest seats and a sense of being close to the action. The ornate furnishings around added a sense of good-old-days nostalgia — a prize fight feeling about the place.

Nostalgia was to play a big part in the revival of boxing in Belfast. In the nineteenth century prize-fights would be held in the little fields that came within yards of Belfast's city centre. In days when pigs were kept in the backyards of houses on the Shankhill and Falls young men like Ike O'Neill Weir (one of the first featherweight champions of the world) were fighting for pennies in the prize ring. And into the twentieth century it had continued, fairground pugilism: "stay with the prize fighter in the ring at the Chapel Fields and win half a crown." While down in the Ulster Hall a veritable army of ex-Chapel Fields boxers fought each other for ten shillings and the Belfast fans became astute students of the science of boxing. McGuigan was to bring a lot of memories flooding back.

The first of McGuigan's fights at the Ulster Hall was against Belgian junior lightweight Jean Marc Renard. He was not believed by the Eastwood camp to be as experienced as he turned out — the twenty-four year old has since fought for the European title and still makes European Boxing Union rankings.

McGuigan was again slow-starting, again over enthusiastic. He was knocked in the seventh, to hit the canvas for the last time so far in his career.

After four rounds Renard was in front, using his left effectively. McGuigan shortened his punches and began to effect some damage on Renard's face. Referee Harry Gibbs scored it 79-78.

"He tried to land a few suicide right handers but settled down and did what he was told," Eddie Shaw said afterwards. From now on McGuigan would do as he was told. Renard was the last man to put McGuigan on the canvas.

Eastwood was intent on getting the best of sparring partners. They included European champion Ken Buchanan. Ken Buchanan was World Lightweight champion between 1970 and 1972, eventually losing the title to McGuigan's hero Roberto Duran.

He earned £2 million from boxing. Through a variety of ill-advised investments he lost most of it. By 1980 he had little left except a thorough knowledge of boxing. Through Paddy Byrne, Eastwood arranged that Buchanan would come to help McGuigan in Belfast.

Buchanan and McGuigan got on well together. "He would talk the teeth off a saw," McGuigan said. "The boy's great gas," Buchanan said.

Buchanan lived in Bangor and sparred with McGuigan. Afterwards they told each other stories, they played pranks, and they had a good time. Buchanan was convinced that McGuigan would go far because of his attitude — no drink, no smoke, no high life.

"In professional boxing you've got to slow everything down. You don't attack the bag, you stay longer on it and you pace yourself. You work on stamina, you keep your strength in reserve," Buchanan says. "It's quite different from amateur boxing." Buchanan was to keep coaching McGuigan not to be overenthusiastic.

After beating Terry Pizarro from Florida after two minutes, twenty-five seconds of the fourth round of his next fight in October, McGuigan maintained that sparring with Buchanan had been more difficult than the fight turned out to be. "I hardly broke into a sweat."

McGuigan worked the left jab to Pizarro's face effectively. "He can be a champion," Pizarro said, "provided they don't push him too hard." McGuigan was in an unusual position in this fight in that referee Bob McWilliam called the boxers together in the second round and asked them to liven it up to give the customers value for money. McGuigan was becoming over-cautious.

The way was clear for a rematch with Eubanks.

The rematch was not just another fight against another workhorse unknown opponent. It was a needle match to excite the punters. Eastwood's Ulster Hall promotions were about to come of age.

This was the chance to put McGuigan's career record back in order. The fight could have been stopped in round six when, after McGuigan had landed two great rights and a left hook, a bell was sounded in the crowd, twenty seconds before the end.

It probably saved Eubanks — but only for two rounds. McGuigan rested in the seventh and his corner asked him for a big last round. The referee stopped it in the eighth after a McGuigan barrage . . . prematurely, many of the crowd thought.

Eubanks reckoned McGuigan had improved fifty per cent since the previous meeting. A clash of heads near the end left McGuigan with a cut eyebrow. Otherwise he was unscathed.

After six fights in seven months, McGuigan married Sandra Mealiff, his sweetheart since the age of thirteen, in December.

The first fight of 1982, a January 27 defeat of Luis de la Sagra from Spain, saw the left hook to the body at its most effective. The referee Bob McMillen scored the fight 80-78½, and de la Sagra went home to nurse his ribs. De la Sagra had lost a European title bout just two months beforehand. This was a prestige victory. People began to discuss McGuigan's British title prospects.

There were two fights in February, 1982. The first was against the declining thirty-year-old, Ian Murray from Manchester. Within a minute, McGuigan had knocked him. It was the first performance by McGuigan at the London-based World Sporting Club.

Then in February, the McGuigan success story entered a new phase. Eastwood's marketing proved successful. McGuigan sold out the Ulster Hall for this first time.

It was unfortunate that the promised opponent, Juan Francisco Rodriguez, former European bantamweight champion, did not show up. A little-known Spaniard, Angel Oliver, was brought along instead. The extra crowds, to fill the 2,500 seats in the hall, were turning up because of McGuigan's capacity for taking opponents out within the distance. Angel Oliver was out of his depth. He struggled for three rounds before he was dumped with a left hook.

Exactly a month later, McGuigan eventually met his first European ranked opponent, junior lightweight Angelo Licata, from Italy. Licata was number seven in Europe and had been beaten twice in twenty-one previous contests. Licata's manager Vincenzo Falzone described McGuigan as a "George Best in gloves" afterwards.

McGuigan had perfected his left jab at this stage. The jab drained Licata completely of energy, knocking wind from his chest, and badly bruising his ribs. Licata was the second victim of McGuigan's left hook to the body, a left hook that had been developed from the time he was sixteen and exploited successfully by Eddie Shaw in the first month after he had turned professional. It was becoming his most famous punch.

Gary Lucas of Liverpool proved to be the first of McGuigan's two first round knockouts. It was Lucas's second defeat inside the distance against McGuigan. In fact the bell sounded when Lucas was being counted out, but the referee ended the contest anyway. Under the rules, it still counts as a knockout. This fight was staged close to McGuigan's home town, in Enniskillen, County Fermanagh.

Six fights in seven months in 1981, six fights in five months in 1982, McGuigan was working hard at getting a lot of experience and quickly.

He was now clearly beyond the stage of the aging workhorses, and into the British and European top ten ranked boxers.

His weight had to be clarified as well, McGuigan became a featherweight, with a nine stone limit in future, rather than the junior lightweight, which allows four pounds more. McGuigan scaled nine stone four pounds for the second Lucas fight and nine stone three and three-quarter pounds for the first Lucas fight and Licata.

Becoming a good professional over the 1981-'82 season was as much a question of confidence as anything else. McGuigan worked out in the Castle Street gym with his sparring partners. He knew little about most of his opponents, just that they had been lined up for him to beat.

His confidence really began to grow when his run of knockouts began in early 1982. The cancelling out of the Eubanks flaw in his pedigree was of immense importance.

After that defeat there was an overriding sense of predestination in each of McGuigan's contests. An opponent would not have been selected if his handlers thought McGuigan might lose. It was McGuigan who was doing the selecting. The masterplan for McGuigan's future must not be upset. At all costs.

This was the old tried and tested bum-a-month formula used all over the world to make a good professional fighter out of a talented amateur. After all, former British featherweight champion Jim "Spider" Kelly from Derry fought 106 times before he challenged for the British title! Rinty Monaghan fought fifty-two times before he became Northern Ireland flyweight champion! Modern-day managers substituted those long gruelling careers for more astute choices of opponents and hiring of sparring partners. As early as the Jean Marc Renard fight in December 1981, McGuigan's fifth, Eastwood had initiated the "spare no expense" policy, and flown in sparring partners to Belfast.

Now McGuigan needed a different style of opponent, and the chance of facing an African came up. The fight was fixed for the World Sporting Club at their Ascot week promotion on June 14 1982. The day remains etched in McGuigan's mind. A young Nigerian mechanic, a champion in his home country where professional boxing is not highly organised, had arrived in Britain to try to make some money and a bit of a name for himself. He fought under the name of Young Ali.

* * * * * * *

6. Fists of Fate

The World Sporting Club was the body which respectabilised boxing in England. A World Sporting Club promotion on Monday June 14 1982, opened the biggest debate on the morals of boxing that Britain has ever known. At the centre of the controversy was Barry McGuigan.

It need just have been a mundane boxing promotion. It was designed to raise money for the Commonwealth Games fund. Barry McGuigan, gold medallist at the previous Commonwealth Games, and Hughie Russell, bronze medallist, would be valuable additions to the programme. Eastwood was approached to let his two medallists fight. He agreed.

The promotion was to be a dress-suit affair. With dinner. At World Sporting Club promotions, gentlemen in evening dress dined while young fighters pounded each other in the ring. The evening dress "dinner and boxing" promotions are regarded as the most reprehensible form of the game by boxing's opponents. It was here that Barry McGuigan delivered the punch which caused Young Ali to die from injuries.

It was a male night, for men talk, and men pursuits. The men spectators were business men with their associates, sportsmen, gamblers who were discussing prospects for the Royal Ascot horse race meeting that week. They wanted good matches, like handicapped races.

This was boxing in an atmosphere far removed from the Ulster Hall, from the howls and chants of Belfast supporters. The sombre surrounding of the Dorchester Hotel on

June 14 1982 saw McGuigan take on another workhorse opponent.

The fights took place in an eerie silence. No "go on ya boyo." Very little idle chat.

McGuigan had fought at one of these promotions already and disliked them, if only for the absence of his close family. Dermot was not there. His father Pat was not there. One uncle came to support him. Even in his amateur days McGuigan had a bigger fan club.

Respectability was the theme of the evening. The guests included Prince Michael of Kent and Captain Mark Phillips, husband of Princess Anne.

Young Ali, Asymin Mustapha to those who knew him, was a late replacement for an English boxer, Steve Farnsworth. Match-maker for the contest, Paddy Byrne, had never even seen him spar.

What they did know was that he was a twenty-three year-old Nigerian, had won eighteen of his twenty fights as a professional, recently lost in the eleventh round against Stix McLeod (Zimbabwe) for the All-African featherweight championship in Lagos, and was pushing a claim to the Commonwealth title, held by Azumah Nelson.

He could be a more difficult opponent than they reckoned. Africans are very durable fighters, usually short on technique, but capable of taking a lot of punishment.

Ali held the West African title, having beaten Raga Murphy from Ghana. Few African fighters ever progress on the world listings that are dominated by the politically minded promoters of South America, the United States, and latterly Asia and Europe. Most Africans come to Europe to pursue their careers.

The fight was virtually ignored as a non-event except for the Irish newspapers. Both McGuigan and Russell were expecting to be nominated for British title eliminators when the new season opened. Both were interrupting their rest period. Both were unsure of how good their opponents were.

Ali had fought very well until the eleventh round of the All-African championship. But there was an overriding feeling of confidence in McGuigan's management. As Tom

Cryan of the *Irish Independent* previewed it: "I find it hard to believe that his handlers would have taken tonight's fight with Young Ali if there was any danger of the masterplan being upset."

Ali wore the Nigerian national colours of (ironically) green, white and orange into the ring and started aggressively, working solid left jabs and fast hooks. In the second the rain of McGuigan punches began. Three rights to the head and a left hook to the body had no effect. A left hook to the jaw had no effect in the fifth. McGuigan was wondering what he had to do to win the fight. He was well ahead on points, yet worried. He had also been warned three times by the referee to keep his punches up. He remarked to Eastwood that no matter what he threw at Ali, the African was able to take his best punches and still come back. Ali backed into McGuigan's corner, then came a right and left to the head, another few blows, and the crushing right uppercut straight to the jaw. The boxer fell on his face, a sign of danger. Ali lay down for thirty seconds.

The crowd wondered whether Ali was likely to beat the count. It never seemed remotely possible. The manager, Guinea Roger, took his boxer in his arms. Ali looked completely dazed as he climbed on wobbly feet and went back to his corner. With the crowd applauding a fine contest he was helped from the ring, still on his feet.

Then he slumped onto the floor on the way to the dressing room and had to be carried, moaning the rest of the way. The applause grew louder, to console the vanquished boxer in his confusion.

Meanwhile in the dressing room McGuigan was thanking everyone who had helped him in his latest win. He talked about his recent injuries and how it was important for him to perform well against Ali. "He was a good fighter. I knew he was wilting. I had him going a few times . . . I was glad to finish him with a right, because some people might think I was injured again."

Doctors flocked around Mustapha administering first aid while he lay semi-conscious for twenty minutes. This was clearly big trouble, he was not just concussed. Someone called for an ambulance. One of the medical men reported that his pulse was fairly strong and that was a good sign.

As the stricken boxer was carried away by ambulance to a Middlesex hospital, the boxing continued.

The *New Statesman* erupted with indignation afterwards: "The circumstances of this tragedy are particularly unattractive — smacking of gladiatorial contests in the Roman Coliseum. The event was a boxing evening promoted by the World Sporting Club — an evening dress affair, where Ascot week revellers enjoyed a night out (complete with brandy and cigars) while being treated to the spectacle of young men, mostly from underprivileged backgrounds, punching one another insensible. Even as Mustapha was being rushed to hospital for his emergency brain operation, the boxing still continued."

Young Ali, Asymin Mustapha was clinically dead within minutes of the fight. Newspaper reporters filing copy immediately from the ringside, were concerned over what they had seen. Tom Cryan's *Irish Independent* report said: "Immediate information was that his pulse was fairly strong and hopes were high that he would recover."

* * * * * * *

7. Trauma

Mustapha was kept on a life support machine in Middlesex for several months. Every evening McGuigan's father rang the hospital for news. Although not a relative, the hospital appreciated the special concern the McGuigans felt and kept them informed that nothing was happening.

There was an attempt by the brain surgeon who operated on Mustapha to meet Pat McGuigan at one stage. The meeting fell through. McGuigan often wonders what might have been said: would it be words of consolation, that Mustapha's condition was not provoked completely by the blow, or instructions that McGuigan would be well advised to give up boxing.

The young Nigerian never regained consciousness. He was moved back to Lagos in November. On December 13, 1982 news came through the Agency wires that Mustapha had died in a Lagos hospital three days earlier.

Mustapha was pronounced clinically dead after two operations failed to relieve pressure on his brain. Boxers die from acute brain trauma, caused by a blow to the head or a heavy fall to the canvas, that results in the brain, moving, twisting and colliding with the skull. If it ruptures the blood vessels that surround it, a hematoma (a heavy build-up of blood) occurs in the narrow space between the rigid skull and the soft brain. It expands and expands and eventually squeezes the brain to death.

Mustapha's position was complicated by the thin skull and a weakness in an artery. Acute brain damage resulted from the combination of the blow and the fall. The family gave permission for the life support machine to be disconnected when it became clear that recovery was not possible.

Mustapha had come to Lagos from rural Nigeria to work as a mechanic. It was two weeks before his wife could be told about the accident.

McGuigan spoke once to Mustapha's wife over the phone. He promised to support her, financially. The British Boxing Board of Control has an insurance scheme for boxing injuries.

The evening of December 13, he should have been celebrating the announcement that he was the new Texaco Sports Star of the Year in boxing. He was now just one fight away from the British featherweight title. Instead he was told by his father that Mustapha had died. The report had come on the wires to the *Irish Times* office. Boxing writer Sean Kilfeather telephoned the McGuigans.

Barry cried a lot. Said he wanted to be alone.

* * * * * * *

8. The Punch

There are some who maintain that McGuigan's boxing

THE PRO GAME

suffered directly as a result of the Mustapha injury. Boxers who have felt the pain of an opponent's death are usually said to be adversely affected in the ring. It rarely affects his aggressiveness. Usually it is reflected in a slight change of technique, or in emphasis.

McGuigan relied on his right uppercut from his first days as a juvenile windmill puncher in Smithboro. The right uppercut beat his first opponents, including Sean Russell.

From the age of sixteen, he worked on more variety in his style. The right uppercut was clearly too predictable for any opponent who watched him in even one bout.

Training in his left hand was one of the hardest parts of McGuigan's training in the 1977-'78 period. But he did it so successfully that he no longer used the left just to set up his right uppercut, but developed a fearsome jab and body-hook that won contests in their own right. The right was rarely used in his early professional career.

Later on there were classic moments when McGuigan got the opening to use his right. The most spectacular was against Levan McGowan in Chicago. Vernon Penprase was landed with a left to the body, and then the right. But the one that shook Asymin Mustapha was the most effective and most spectacular right of all.

In the eerie silence of the World Sporting Club promotion the thump of that right was loud, resounding, echoing. The impact was clear to all the spectators almost immediately. When Mustapha fell forward, that impact was compounded. Newspaper reports the following day, still unaware of the extent of the tragedy that they had witnessed, described that as the best punch of McGuigan's career, amateur or professional.

The right has always been McGuigan's great untapped talent. He liked to loop it, and therefore lose some of its impact, often missing the target at the same time when he was an amateur. When it was presented with one short slamming uppercut (all it needed to travel was twelve inches) it was devastating.

There are those who maintain that McGuigan never used the right to the same effect after the Mustapha fight.

9. Double Crisis

McGuigan faced not one but two crises over the death of Asymin Mustapha. He went back into the ring in October and again in November 1982 as he sought eliminators for the British title. Then came the real crisis after Mustapha died in December.

The questions about why it had happened managed to avoid discussing the morality of the sport itself. The British Boxing Board of Control was urged to introduce brain scans. One of the first victims of the new regulation was a Donegal boxer with the Eastwood stable, Stephen Friel, who was refused permission to fight in January 1984 because he did not have the results of a brain scan.

The debate was so strong that by the end of 1983 some Americans were conceding that Britain would, eventually, follow Norway and Sweden in banning boxing. The British, Canadian and American Medical Associations all called for boxing to be banned.

Mustapha was the first British boxing casualty in twelve years. It came close on the heels of the death of Welsh boxer Johnny Owens in America and the televised deaths in the United States of Willie Classen and Korean Duk Koo Kim. In calling for boxing to be banned, the British Medical Association described it as "legalised Grevious Bodily Harm".

The British Boxing Board of Control stood its ground. Ali should not have boxed because of his thin skull casing and artery weakness, an aneurysm.

But in January 1983 the BBBC reduced the length of its title fights from fifteen rounds to a concessionary twelve. The World Boxing Council followed suit, under medical pressure.

There was not much to talk about after the death of Mustapha. McGuigan did not decide to retire from boxing immediately, but after a few days he had made up his mind to do so.

When Hugh Russell, his friend and colleague won the British bantamweight title on January 25 1983, McGuigan did not even attend. His mother, Katie, was glad. She welcomed McGuigan back to the shop to work, to help out, and although there was not a lot of work for him, she thought that maybe her son could work out something to support him.

McGuigan felt confident that his name in the newspaper headlines for so long would help him find a job. He might get generous terms to start up a business of his own, now that he was well known.

His wife Sandra worked in a launderette. She was pregnant with his child. McGuigan became more and more aware of the fact that she was supporting him over the weeks.

The family grocery shop provided them with food. The fiercely independent McGuigan was beginning to think of returning to boxing.

When Eastwood rang at first, McGuigan would not even talk to him over the phone. He was still bound by a three year contract. He expected that relations with Eastwood would be strong enough for the manager to waive the remaining part of the contract. But he was also aware that Eastwood strongly believed that the right thing for him to do was to get back into the ring.

McGuigan spoke to his parents, his clergymen, and his wife. Even to them, he spoke little for long periods.

He found comfort in his religious beliefs. He prayed.

There were plenty of reasons to justify returning to the ring. One was the contract that he should be duty-bound to fulfill.

Another was the fact that, had the tables been turned, would Mustapha have reacted the same way? Would he have become a manic depressive, thinking about what he had done all the time? McGuigan doubted it.

A third was the fact that McGuigan was not at fault — the fault lay in the inadequate brain scanning of boxers before a fight.

And the overwhelming reason of all was the economic one. McGuigan's pregnant wife was supporting him. The only thing he knew anything about was boxing. So McGuigan boxed again. To win the British title.

While the sport was being debated, so was the image of Barry McGuigan. Eastwood did not want it mentioned when his boxer was interviewed afterwards. With each subsequent success, McGuigan's story always carried an addendum questioning the morals of boxing. It was a lot of pressure on a twenty-one year-old.

Sean Kilfeather, who broke the news of Mustapha's death to the family, wrote in January 1983: "If McGuigan retires from boxing both he and Asymin Mustapha will be forgotten. But if McGuigan continued in his craft the tragedy that has befallen him will be a constant reminder to all of us and an appeal that safer boxing is required. He owes himself and his family and another family in Lagos that kind of memorial."

It did not matter that most of the ringside reporters had confronted the moral question a long time ago and decided in favour of boxing. In each profile of McGuigan the death had to be mentioned. Kilfeather, of the *Irish Times*, summed up the feelings of the ringsiders when he spoke in April 1983 about "the moral climate which finds boxing less acceptable than nuclear armaments."

For those outside the sport, the death remained paramount. How could McGuigan get back into the ring after that experience, they asked?

The answer is with difficulty. Before the analysts began to contextualise his World championship victory in terms of the death of Mustapha, McGuigan did it for them in two simple tearful sentences after the Pedroza fight:

"One thing. I've been thinking about it all week. And I said if I won this World title I would dedicate it to the young lad that died when he fought me in 1982. And I said I would like it to be not just an ordinary fighter that beat him but . . . the World champion."

It was not just the two sentences. It was the emotion behind the delivery. In the hour of triumph.

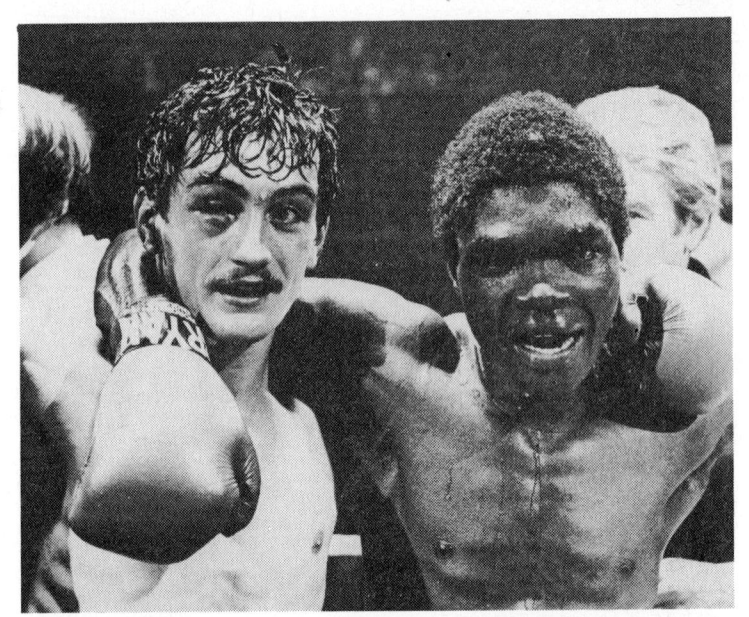

Relief: McGuigan with damaged eye and defeated opponent Charm Chiteule, the most worrying of his post-title contests.

Triumph: British title challenger Clude Ruan takes a count.

CHAPTER 5

Hero

*"Barry, you don't fight like a white man,
you fight like a brother."*
— Tony Santana after watching a
McGuigan-Vinnie Costello sparring war.

1. The British Title

In 1983 and 1984 McGuigan rose quickly from being just another boxer to being a world contender. He achieved it in seven spectacular stages.

In April 1983 he won the British title in Belfast against Vernon Penprase.

In October 1983 he won the European title, knocking Gregorio Natin out in the sixth round.

In January 1984 he became the top Commonwealth title contender by defeating Charm Chiteule with a close and worrying tenth round knockout.

In April 1984 he became a world ranked boxer by beating Jose Caba.

In June 1984 he made his American television debut by stopping Paul De Vorce in the sixth round.

In October 1984 he beat Filippe Orozco in another televised encounter.

Finally he showed he was ready for the World title in February 1985 by beating former champion Juan Laporte.

Mustapha was not dead when McGuigan climbed back into the ring in October 1982, some three months after the Ali fight. But he was still in a coma in a London hospital, depending on a life support machine. The boxing public regarded the whole incident as a boxing death.

The fight was lined up against Sammy Meck, a French-based Cameroons African. That arrangement fell through, and instead McGuigan fought Jimmy Duncan, a top ten-rated British featherweight. This was one of the chances he had waited for to get an eliminator for the vacant British featherweight title, abandoned by Pat Cowdell who had gone in search of bigger things.

Had he fought Meck the task might not have been as easy. The following May against Meck, the African proved as durable as Mustapha and required seventeen punches to put him down. McGuigan's comeback was hardly the place to exert force or volume like that.

McGuigan opened a cut over Duncan's eye, and the Liverpudlian retired at the end of the fourth round. He had been on his knees during the fourth after a right hook to the body.

Of even greater significance was the fact that the 2,500 seats in the Ulster Hall were all sold out. McGuigan was a sell-out for the first time.

McGuigan got his eliminator. It was against Paul "Bad Boy" Huggins of Hastings, an older fighter with a fifteen-match undefeated record.

Referee James Brinnell of Wales stepped between the contenders as McGuigan unleashed a flurry of blows at the end of the fifth and stopped the contest. The crowd wanted it to go on. Huggins wanted it to go on but for a different reason. The crowd sensed a knock-out was due.

McGuigan supporters had chanted "easy, easy" earlier on. Huggins' manager Dave Harris shouted out that the referee was a "bloody disgrace". Afterwards in the Forum Hotel he told everyone that cared to listen that they had been robbed, or at least deprived of a fair chance of finishing the contest properly and without argument.

The crowd chanted "Sims is next, Sims is next." Eastwood beamed at the adulation his boxer was receiving. He had taken time off to instruct the girls to parade around with the placard giving the number of the round. From now on, everything was to be done to perfection.

Crowds tried to get in the toilet windows at the Ulster Hall. Eastwood was thinking of a bigger venue, bigger purse offers, bigger money.

McGuigan sat in his dressing room with a monk-like cowl over his head and confessed to enjoying the fight. "Like my amateur days," he said. In more ways than one. It was like his slow-starting amateur days, when he ran out of rounds at the end of three. McGuigan clearly lost the first round against Huggins.

"I went through my entire repertoire tonight," he said. Then he turned to the journalists and said: "Can you spell that?" This was vintage, relaxed McGuigan. As one journalist observed, "Not only did he know all the answers, he knew all the questions as well!"

And he was sad. "The referee was right to stop it. Maybe if the referee had stopped another fight a bit earlier Young Ali would not be clinically dead today."

On April 12 1983 McGuigan ended his novice days. He beat baby-faced Vernon Penprase from Plymouth to win the vacant British title, to the delight of the Ulster Hall audience of 2,500. His first comment? "I want to win the European title and the World title."

McGuigan had lost five days of training because of pneumonia. Yet he floored Penprase after just two minutes and fifty seconds of the second round.

Against Penprase, McGuigan was 1/4 favourite. The tickets were sold out in forty-eight hours.

The initial arrangement was for a fight on February 22. Eastwood bid £17,500 for the fight. There was no possibility of providing that figure from gate receipts alone. Trevor McLintock of Smirnoff stepped in with sponsorship and McGuigan had a home town setting for his British title defence.

McGuigan was number two challenger for the title at the time, held by Steve Sammy Sims. Sims vacated his title, rather than fight McGuigan to take on Loris Stecca for the European title. McGuigan was nominated to take on the third ranked Vernon Penprase. Terry McKeown, whom Sims had beaten for the vacant British title (later European champion Charlie Magri was previous holder) had retired. McGuigan and Penprase were left.

From the ring McGuigan made his way up a flight of stairs to an exuberant dressing room. Thank you, thank you, thank you, he gave the little litany of trainer, family, people, press, doormen, whatever, that was to become more and more familiar each time. He talked about greater honours ahead. And if he made it the praise would go to his wife, to his family, to his friends and to this marvellous Ulster Hall crowd.

Even his opponent was thanked: "Vernon (Penprase) was not in a position to defend himself and I admire him for his courage. He was very generous in his praise afterwards."

Penprase was hurt. He asserted that he had never been hit so hard in his life. "I have been hit by good one-shot punchers in the past, but Barry is consistently hard. It's a mug's game to carry on in second rate halls after meeting someone like McGuigan.

The sequence of events in the fight had been uncomplicated. A good old-fashioned, crowd-pleasing siege of punches that had Penprase in trouble from the first round on. Left jabs, right hooks, right uppercuts... the McGuigan plan had been to jab for four rounds. It did not even take that long. The relentless jab continued in the second round. Blood was creeping from Penprase's nose.

Then came a left hook, not a hard left hook. Penprase was worried about McGuigan's low punching. He complained to the referee twice during the fight. Then came an unsettling thumb in the eye. He blinked, a perfectly natural reaction, his father maintained afterwards. The left hook caught him unawares. "It wasn't hard," McGuigan said afterwards. "It just must have caught him in the right place."

Penprase went down, came up in three seconds and then came the chase.

Penprase sought cover in the eighteen-foot ring. He was caught in the opposite corner. A shattering left hook to the jaw bobbed Penprase against the bottom rope. It almost sent him through the gap between two of the ropes.

Then referee Harry Gibbs cried halt. He put a paternal

arm around Penprase and guided him to a corner.

Manager and father, Tony Penprase declared immediately after the fight on television that McGuigan would be world champion within two years. He was wrong. It took two years and two months.

The jab was like a ramrod, he recalls. The only options in fighting McGuigan were to get on your bike, jab and move ceaselessly, or to get in and slug it out toe to toe. Either way, he said, we would lose. Penprase had boxed 135 times, twenty-five times as a professional. He had promised his father he would retire as soon as he was knocked down or stopped. He had been beaten six times previously, most notably a morale destroying points loss to Steve Sims in June 1981. He had encountered nothing like McGuigan ever before.

While Penprase announced his retirement, "I don't want to be a trial horse," McGuigan was hearing from the boxing ringside reports that he had ended the fight with a right. He did not know that. He automatically followed his left jab with a right. It was almost a reflex blow.

The British title had been worth £2,500 to McGuigan, £2,500 to Penprase. Penprase got £150 for television rights. His father still feels upset, that the fee was so low, and that the fight has been shown forty-three times since. Penprase being floored by that right, again and again and again, the only fight that will live on in boxing memory after a twenty-five fight career that brought seventeen successes.

* * * * * * *

2. A Bridge To The South

Winning the British title opened new markets to the Eastwoods. Now they had a champion to market, not just another Saturday evening music hall boxer. The British newspapers took the Clones man to heart. Three big marketing points appealed to them immediately, the articulate nature of this young white and good-looking boxer and the peace dimension to the Ulster Hall boxing attendances.

The first salvoes on the Eastwoods side were fired by the Fleet Street press who lamented that so far, BBC television in the neighbouring isle had not shown McGuigan. The station was condemned for being parochial. McGuigan was exciting and attractive enough a fighter to justify their taking pictures from the Ulster Hall.

The British dimension had been successfully catered for. Now Dublin had to be looked after. Eastwood staged a press conference at the Shelbourne Hotel where he announced a boxing show in Navan against Cameroons boxer, Paris-based Sammy Meck. Navan had previously been the venue for a 1982 boxing promotion organised by the Christles. It had a 4,000 capacity show hall, was cheaper than similar venues in Dublin, and was reasonably accessible from both Dublin and Clones. The theme of the press conference was that this was a special gesture to the Clones fans, requested by McGuigan and benevolently agreed to by Mr Eastwood.

Eastwood maintained that Dublin was a professional boxing wasteland. European title fights in 1980 and 1981 involving Derry boxer Charlie Nash had flopped. He was reluctant to move away from the tried-and-trusted ground of Belfast. But just this once . . . .

In fact McGuigan had promised this to the Clones supporters club, then numbering about 400. All of the previous five Ulster Hall fights had been sold out and McGuigan promised this for local people who had been unable to get tickets.

He turned down an offer to box on the Bobby Chachon -v- Boza Edwards World Boxing Title bill in Las Vegas to do so. Eastwood apparently turned down several offers for McGuigan to box in Las Vegas between 1983 and 1985.

Meck was a powerful fighter, and had forced a draw in Madrid with Pedroza's predecessor as World Featherweight boxing champion Cecilio Lastra. He had been initially proposed as a McGuigan opponent in the October 1982 comeback bout at the Ulster Hall.

Meck was the victim of a very dubious decision in his fight against European featherweight champion Loris

Stecca in Rimini — again a draw. Meck's manager had been in touch with the European Boxing Union to grant final eliminator status to this contest, so that his boxer would get a crack at Stecca.

Africans, McGuigan maintains, are the most durable type of fighter. Meck proved durable all right — it took seventeen punches to fell him. In the end the fight went six rounds and the ringsiders were spattered with blood. The promotion was not a sell-out. Eastwood's lack of faith in Dublin boxing promotions had been justified.

Eastwood is said to have lost £2,000 to £3,000 on Navan. McGuigan got paid less than £1,000 for his appearance. The venue was empty at 2.30, the bulk of the attendance only began to file into the building at 3.30.

But an important link had been forged with the Irish Republic soon after McGuigan had won the British title. Bridges, carefully built, had to be maintained constantly in good working order.

The Navan fight had not quelled the Eastwoods' pioneering spirit. The tour was to continue to the United States where the offers to fight in Las Vegas had come just a few months before.

* * * * * * *

3. America

The lure of the dollar offered a chance to explore further areas for the Eastwoods. An entourage that included Eddie Shaw, Paddy Byrne, Eastwood, McGuigan and Dermot McGuigan set off to America with the hope of some major billing fights in mid 1983.

It was a move calculated to stimulate Irish American interest in McGuigan just as he was on the brink of the bigtime. It did not really succeed, as McGuigan had only one fight, and not much attention was paid to the new British champion. Even European champions do not carry much stature in the United States, who concern themselves with their home boxers, and Latin Americans and later, rather disdainfully, with Europeans and Asians. McGuigan was a nobody.

The Irish-American market had been exploited so successfully by American third generation fighters with large shamrocks on their togs even the authenticity of McGuigan did not break through the barriers. Americans were so used to "Fighting Irishmen" that even English boxers were often mistaken for them. Marvin Hagler once described Britain's Alan Minter as "the last of the big-mouthed Irishmen."

Gerry Cooney and Sean O'Grady had made a lot of money from being Irish in recent years. Being *really* Irish did not count for as much.

But Eastwood's second motive was based on his policy of "getting the right sparring partners". Flying McGuigan to the sparring partners was infinitely more sensible than flying the sparring partners to Belfast. McGuigan spent a lot of time in New York, Atlantic City and Chicago gyms. From the Americans he could learn the real trade of world class fighting.

McGuigan, Eastwood and Eddie Shaw made their way to Gleason's Gym, near the junction of West 30th Street and Eighth Avenue in Manhattan, looking for experience. The gym, founded by an Italian, had become famous as the home gym of Gerry Cooney and countless other champions. Round the corner from Madison Square Gardens, it represented the centre of the New York boxing world.

McGuigan sparred there against Vinnie Costello, whose brother Billy was later to become World Junior Lightweight champion. The two began to hit harder and harder. Tony Santana, another boxer who sparred with McGuigan told the newcomer from Ireland: "Barry, you don't fight like a white man. You fight like a brother."

Bobby McQuillar saw McGuigan in this bout. He decided that here was a future champion. So too did Alex Wallec, the ABC television boxing buyer. McGuigan was a definite prospect, he thought. No single sparring session in McGuigan's career was to prove as important as that against Costello.

Costello shrugs away the performance. He hurt Costello, so Costello hit him back. The spar became a battle of wits. As good as any Madison Square Garden Felt forum promotion bout.

McQuillar was to assume great importance in the development of McGuigan's career. A man who had beaten Sandy Saddler, but who refused to play ball with the Mafia and consequently never got a title chance (it was common for mobsters to ask boxers to throw a contest to get reward in those days), McQuillar had trained all the greats, Muhammad Ali, Sugar Ray Robinson, Macho Camacho. McGuigan was to be added to his very impressive clientele.

McQuillar came into Gleason's Gym in the middle of the sparring session. "He had Vinnie Costello in the ring and he was kicking his butt. I said hey, who's this fighter. They told me he was some guy from Ireland. I said hey, he's going to be the next Irish champion. I say Ireland hasn't had a champion for thirty years. Barry's going to be the next one. I knew that. I just knew it."

"He had something. He had one punch over that liver. That liver punch, the left hook to your liver, he could do that better than anyone I ever seen." I thought that was about the best punch he had."

European fighters do not count for much in the American boxing world. Nevertheless McQuillar was impressed. McGuigan was a European who could make it.

"It's not the European fighters that are at fault. It's the trainers. The trainers have a lot to do with it. You just can't stay back in the old ways. You just can't do it like Joe Louis did it. Like Ray Robinson did it. This is a new day. This is a new era. A new generation. Man, you got to get down with the modern times. Everything modernises itself. You just can't stay back in 1910. You gotta get with it."

"My thing is the element of surprise. Another thing is defence. If a man's got a good defence and he knows he can protect himself, it makes him bold."

McQuillar pauses now and narrows his eyes for effect. "And the bolder you are, out there, the better you are."

It really comes down to common sense. "Even before

he was a champion, he was living like a champion," McQuillar recalls. "I admired the young man. He was living like a champion. He was taking care of his family like he should. He wasn't running round. He wasn't after women. He wasn't this. He wasn't that. I knew that the possibility of him being champion was made that much greater."

"His discipline reminded me of my own. I was a disciplined fighter. You could see it. He wanted it."

McGuigan also sparred with Harlem-raised Rick Young at Gleason's Gym. "The fact about sparring with Barry is the pressure that he puts on you. The pace. The man got real pace.

"And condition — the fact that he can keep coming without getting tired. When the other guy gets tired he's just coming on. That's very difficult to cope with."

McGuigan learned about developing his already American-style crouch. He learned about elbow work, the elbows that strayed outwards were soon strapped in. He learned to cope with elbows that brushed and clamped at close quarters, that deflected body punches, that unsettled.

Eastwood was trying to impress promoters in the way McGuigan was impressing trainers. He wanted fights for his boy. A cut eye sustained against Sammy Meck counted McGuigan out of a Madison Square Garden Felt forum promotion on June 16. Instead there was talk about appearing on bills organised by Don King, Bob Arum, and Frankie Gello. Nothing happened.

Instead Mickey Duff arranged a fight on a promotion by Cedric Kushaner, a South African who had promoted World Heavyweight champion Gerry Coetzee. Kushaner was organising a bill in the Da Vinci Stadium in Chicago. He had Frank Bruno and McGuigan on the card as visiting European champions. The emphasis was on a local television cable station, Sports Vision, and about 400 people filled the half empty room. The rest was filled with television personnel and cables.

The opponent La Von McGowan, a boxer from Davinport, Iowa, who turned professional a year earlier, had lost, drawn and won in his three fights, and was immediately dropped from the Ring Record book. McGuigan produced a fierce right to knock him out in the first round.

Kushaner was impressed. He offered McGuigan a fight in Chicago on Irish Jackie Collins' bill in April 1984. Another offer came to fight on the Hagler-Duran bill in November. But McGuigan had learned enough. It was time to come home.

McGuigan sparred with twenty different featherweights and lightweights in fourteen days. It cost £15,000 of Eastwood money, with precious little in return for the fight against McGowan, but in terms of sparring experience the camp maintained it was well worth it.

Simms had proved elusive. McGuigan was nominated for a fight against Simms in March 1983. Simms meanwhile had been nominated for a European title fight. Stephen Eastwood threatened to bring Simms to court to honour his contract to fight McGuigan. Simms is said to have turned down an offer of a £9,000 purse in Belfast. Simms would prefer to take £2,000 to fight in Wales, Eastwood claimed.

* * * * * * *

4. Back To Europe

Eastwood sought a European title fight against featherweight champion Loris Stecca from Rimini. He wanted to bring Stecca to Belfast and get a prestige victory. The European Boxing Union ordered Stecca to meet McGuigan. Stecca baulked at the prospect. He was seeking a world title fight, on the basis of his European record.

Stecca too proved elusive. A match against Stecca in March 1982 had fallen through. McGuigan was nominated by the European Boxing Union (the most vigilant boxing authority in the world as regards looking after the interests of challengers) on January 13 1982. The managers had until February 20 to make a match. After that it was up to purse offers.

There was a chance that Eastwood could negotiate a Stecca fight until August 6. Eastwood was determined that the fight would come to the King's Hall, a venue with a seating capacity far greater than anything he had handled so far. He set out the cost of the King's Hall experiment, £70,000, a fortune by the standards of previous boxing promotions in Belfast. On August 31, Stephen Eastwood went to Italy to bid in the purse offer game.

A fight-off for the vacant title with Stecca's compatriot, Valerio Nati seemed more likely.

The final fight before the challenge for the European title was to be against Reuben Herasme of the Dominican Republic, who had seventeen wins and four draws in twenty-two professional fights.

The original opponent was Hector Sanchel. The British Boxing Board of Control objected to a fight against Sanchel. They wrote to Eastwood:

"In view of McGuigan's punching power and the ease with which he demolished his last ten opponents in thirty-two rounds of boxing, the ease with which he won the British title and the first round knockdown of Lavon McGowan in Chicago, we will only sanction an opponent of more experience than Hector Sanchel and one who has participated against World rated opponents."

The sub was Ruben Herasme, managed by Lou Barski and from the stable of Felix Zambala.

Herasme did not complete the second round against McGuigan. A left over Herasme's guard set the pattern in the first round. Another volley was fired in the second when Herasme sent a left to the head and a right to the body and then came a left to the ribs that smothered and choked the visitor. He tried to get up, and rolled over in a bundle.

Around the ring they said it was his most devastating performance. Eleven fights, thirty-four rounds, what average did you say? The European title looked more likely than ever. Beating Herasme looked like it had just been arranged to boost the ticket sales.

Eastwood and Trevor McClintock, a close business associate and friend, and the man behind Smirnoff's sponsorship of McGuigan's fights considered the risk involved in moving fights from the 2,500 capacity Ulster Hall to the 7,000 capacity King's Hall.

McClintock said yes. Eastwood took the gamble. Tickets were sold out for the dearest and cheapest sections of the King's Hall before the big night. Those on the gallery were snapped up at £10 each. A couple of dozen ground-level £12 tickets were on sale at the door. The promotion was a success. So was the fight.

* * * * * * *

5. Fighting Nati

European title day began at eight o'clock in Jean Anderson's guesthouse in Bangor, when McGuigan woke, uncomfortable and tense. The process of dehydration before the weigh-in is the most trying part of a boxer's fight build-up. By the time he had dozed off again it was time to go.

The weigh-in at the Forum hotel passed without a hitch. McGuigan weighed in at nine stone on the button — the featherweight limit. He declined a number of interviews and headed back to Bangor to eat.

The last meal before the fight is designed towards restoring fatty and carbohydrate foods into the system. Sandra had concocted just the right type of meal, mince steak, peas, onions and mushrooms. Plenty of grease.

Then came ice cream, lots of it. And chocolate. A half mile walk, just for the fresh air, and back to bed. Eight hours to go.

McGuigan was up again at six to drink tea, coffee and hot milk. A short rest in bed followed. He was up again at half seven for a cold shower. The real preparation began.

The boxer's version of war paint, the grease was put on. He travelled to the King's Hall in the Eastwood Rolls Royce, put on boots, bandages, track suit, and gloves, and lay down to wait for the Moment.

In the distance he could hear the crowd, but still did not realise the extent of what he was walking into. There was one slight hitch in that the tapes over his hands were reckoned not to be high enough towards the knuckles for a European title fight. But that was the only hitch.

Only one of the six fights in the build-up went the full length. McGuigan was ready. The crowd was ready. He prayed. And he commenced the thirty-yard walk from the dressing room to the ring.

The King's Hall was built in 1934 by the Royal Ulster Society. A venue for exhibitions, concerts and boxing matches. It was re-roofed with an encased steel roof in 1981. The acoustics created by the new roof was largely responsible for the phenomenal atmosphere as the boxers entered the ring.

Seven thousand places had been filled. McGuigan's career had entered a new phase.

The crowd chanted and clapped. The rolling sound of Rocky theme music came over the loudspeakers. Two Ultra Arc blue radiation spotlights lit the passage to the ring. The crowd had been waiting since six o'clock, when the queues stretched down the Lisburn Road, lapping the walls around Malone Presbyterian Church. They had come to see Larmour from the Shankill and McGuigan from Clones box for their titles. They cheered them both. But McGuigan's was the prestige fight.

The reporters noted the angle. Falls and Shankill.

It was almost audacious for the Italian to pin McGuigan against the ropes in the second round. But already McGuigan's body punches were hurting. At the start of the third round Nati was to his feet before the bell. He was bluffing. McGuigan's strength was taking its toll.

Nati fought back. He connected with McGuigan's head and was gaining confidence when McGuigan's punches were judged to be too low. This is what McGuigan was to call the Bob Hope syndrome.

"Your togs are only supposed to come up to your navel. His were way above that! It's like Bob Hope in the film where he pulled his shorts way over his face, cut out two slits for his eyes and said — no hitting below the belt."

The low punches were a contentious issue. Twice McGuigan was warned officially. West German referee Kurt Halbach might have disqualified him in another ring in another town. "He's trying to get us back for what happened in Hamburg," said one punter refreshed with news of Northern Ireland's 1-0 soccer victory over the Germans earlier in the day. In the howling King's Hall, disqualification was unthinkable.

McGuigan was told by his corner to try the right uppercut. Then try the right hand, step back and hit him one-two as he was coming in. But it was dangerous to open up against Nati.

Nati tried to finish it in the fifth round. Eddie Shaw advised Barry "when you hit him the one-two step back and try the one-two again." Barry was finding the gloves very slippy. His body-punching was suffering. Nati came prepared for a great body puncher. He blocked everything.

The sixth round was to be McGuigan's rest round. McGuigan wasn't trying to break Nati's defence with anything like the same fervour. Then one of his body punches hit Nati right on target. The fight was over.

That killer blow was an uppercut. McGuigan followed up with a double left hook. He rushed in to try another uppercut but Nati was down. Three seconds before the end of round six Nati was counted out.

* * * * * * *

6. "There's no point in reaching for the ceiling."

The celebrations were memorable. The party was portable, which was just as well. McGuigan's dressing room was a modest thirty-by-fifteen-foot room and hardly appropriate for a European Featherweight Champion's celebrations. Furthermore it was choc-a-bloc with friends and associates. Most would be departing for Belfast's Forum Hotel or following the boxer to Clones.

Barney Joe Eastwood purred and smiled. He was full of quotables. They chipped off at first. Then they began to roll. Finally they all swept out like an avalanche. Or McGuigan going for the kill.

It was not because of the champagne he was sipping. It was the ecstasy, the relief, the sheer sense that now he could relax, the night had been just what he had dreamed, and the critics who said two years ago that he would never fill the King's Hall were proven wrong.

"It has always been my dream to stage a World Title fight. Now I'm fifty-one, and it's too late, but maybe my son . . . I would love to do it for the lovely people of Northern Ireland. Who would ever think there were any troubles in Northern Ireland to look at the crowd out there tonight . . . He was never off the bit as we say in horse racing . . . Boxing is my life, my fun, and I'm really enjoying it . . . The guy that outbids us for a World Title fight is going to have an awful lot of dough."

Interviewer after interviewer was impressed by his infectious excitement.

"What we need is a stick. Someone Barry can beat. But he must be in the top ten in the world!"

In the corner Barry too was talking incessantly, anxious wife at his side, sleeping bag across his legs and trunks, sitting up on a table with his back supported like a war veteran.

For him there was no champagne. He sipped Coca Cola from a paper cup, signed posters, said hello to half of Clones, some of Bangor, family, friends, acquaintances, old boxers, boxing folk. Nobody's word was scorned or rejected. Nobody was refused. The champ had time.

"The crowd were fantastic. I'd like to thank my fellow professionals — Dave, Hughie." Part boxer, part MC to the whole ceremonial of victory in the dressing rooms, Barry's high pitched voice rang out. "My wife, my family they were great.

"I'm ready to work my way to the top," he said. To be World champion. "There's no point in reaching for the ceiling. Reach for the sky and you'll get to the ceiling. Reach for the ceiling and you'll get nowhere."

What had made the difference? "I think the trip to the States, and Eddie would agree with me, was beneficial. I've been trying outside stepping and hustling on my feet instead of leaving myself as a straight target. I was trying to hustle, and shift to the side . . . shift to the side. So that I was never a static target. I was always moving.

"I was trying to keep relaxed. It was difficult. He was

on top of me from the start. But I was only starting to go. I felt fantastic. I hadn't shifted into third yet. He's not like the typical Italian at all."

It was new surroundings for a new occasion. A bit of a dream for McGuigan, a bit of a nightmare for the declining Italian.

Now twenty-seven, he had been a professional since April 1978, having turned pro just before his twenty-second birthday. He had held the European Bantamweight title from December 1980 to April 1982, defending against Vincente Rodriguez, British champion John Feeney, France's Jean-Jacques Souris, and McGuigan opponents Luis de la Sagra and Esteban Eguia. He lost the title and drew a rematch with Giuseppe Fosatti. Because of weight problems, he moved up to featherweight, and had been stopped in twelve rounds by Loris Stecca.

Stecca had bigger ambitions. So Nati had what amounted to his last chance against McGuigan.

Nati's dressing room had a little female figure on the door to denote its use on normal nights. Seven barking Italians occupied it tonight. No spika English. Nobody. A hasty interview was conducted in franglais.

Quatre times McGuigan had hit too low. The referee did not see. It hurt. Nati got cramps. McGuigan was too strong. Stronger than anyone else Nati had fought. Stecca? Stecca *comme ca* (hand held at waist height), McGuigan COMME CA (hand held above head height). And an accomplice held up fingers to denote how long a Stecca-McGuigan fight would last. He only used one hand.

Stecca *did* get his ambition, by shedding a few pounds. He became WBA Junior Featherweight champion for a short period in 1984, and then was rated number three challenger (five according to *Ring* magazine) in the division. He has also crept back into the European rankings at featherweight as chief challenger to McGuigan's title.

* * * * * * *

7. The Stick

McGuigan was now European champion. But his victory

over Nati had precious little impact on the World ratings. To fight a World champion, he had to be rated in the top ten in the world. Eastwood needed a stick, someone Barry could beat.

There were other options, the traditional Belfast route of becoming Commonwealth champion. Within two months of winning the European title, McGuigan was paired with top Commonwealth challenger Charm Chiteule. He overtrained and over-sparred before the fight. It almost cost him dear in the end.

The fight took place in January, on a frosty night. Consequently there were empty seats at the back of the King's Hall.

Chiteule was twenty-nine and an inch shorter than McGuigan at five-feet-six-inches. He was also largely an unknown quantity, having boxed in the United States and Germany, as well as his native Lusaka since 1981, when he last appeared in London. His victories included a second round knock-out of former World featherweight champion Celilio Lastra. He had been ahead of Azumah Nelson on points when he was knocked out in their fight for the Commonwealth title in 1982. The prize was number one contender's place for the Commonwealth title.

Backstage there was an air of detached anticipation.

"Chiteule's coming in five minutes, then Barry." Outside Rinty Monaghan was being applauded. Chiteule went out. Applause, even rapturous applause greeted him. Then came a group of twelve. The pushers-out-of-the-way, the bagmen, Eddie Shaw, Eastwood, McGuigan shadow boxing. The little train stopped inside the door. The Rocky music was starting. Manager Eastwood cried halt.

Bouncers in bow ties gesticulated madly through peep holes in the door. Hold it, hold it, hold it! Eastwood raced away and returned with a small iron gadget, for cut eyes. The little procession was put back into order. McGuigan entered the King's Hall to an almighty din.

It was a vital moment. McGuigan won the fight, but with a badly bruised eye. His swollen eye meant he had been one-eyed and one-sided since the fourth round. He was restricted, worried, and relieved to have come through this test. His famous body punches had been deflected by Chiteule's elbows (downwards, he lamented afterwards). He could not afford to use his right for six rounds — another punch to the eye would have been fatal. His right hand was used as a guard, in defence instead of attack.

Instead McGuigan battled and battled until Chiteule tired. It took ten rounds, until a prolonged barrage of punches really hurt the Zambian for the first time. The referee, Ronald Dakin, stopped the fight.

"I had loads left, I hadn't started," McGuigan said from his bed of blankets in the dressing room. And he demanded a new rule to have the thumb stitched into the boxing gloves. Chiteule's thumb had closed his eye. "I never hit that guy with my best punches."

"Tough bastard," was Eddie Shaw's verdict. Barry took the hand of Chiteule's trainer when he came into the room, cocked his one good eye to emphasise the sincerity of what he was about to say, and said lowly "good fighter."

The purists worried a little about Barry's low punching. McGuigan confessed that, yes, once he had hit too low. He had apologised. Someone put it gently to Eastwood that anywhere else, McGuigan might have been disqualified. Eastwood said nonsense. Chiteule had pushed McGuigan's punches downwards with his elbow.

Then came mention of a new opponent. Jose Caba — world rated, stayed the distance with Caba, a name to conjure with. A 60,000 dollar purse, venue didn't matter, wherever they could get the most dough, crowds don't mean a thing, television was what counted. It could be Belfast, it might be Atlantic City, Las Vegas, any gambling town. Who knows?

The television game was about to begin.

* * * * * * *

8. Caba

American television networks are only interested in top ten, exciting fighters. McGuigan was exciting, but he was still only European champion. Mickey Duff worked hard to interest the American in taking a show from Belfast. He talked about the exciting young Belfastman, that could unite Catholic and Protestant, about his bobbing, weaving, plundering style, and about the earsplitting atmosphere of the King's Hall.

Duff brought tapes of McGuigan's fights to the three major broadcasting networks in the United States. High-paying television network Home Box Office screen only a dozen fights a year, all of them in peak time. McGuigan was clearly not in their league yet.

ABC television spend their budget sparingly, and only screen championship fights. Occasionally they make an exception for a younger boxer of whom a lot is expected, like an Olympic Gold medallist. But they were not a market for McGuigan.

CBS television are said to have as high a boxing budget as ABC, and they spend more of it on relatively unknown fighters for afternoon sports programme time.

The fourth station, NBC, were most excited about McGuigan. They liked the image. In American television's quick-fire advertising-conscious world, it is important to explain to viewers exactly why an up-and-coming boxer like McGuigan should be worthy of viewing time. Both NBC and CBS toyed with the prospect of a three-minute feature on this peace-making lad from Belfast to promote their programme.

The telling factor in buying boxing matches is not money, but dates. NBC dropped out. CBS could not manage the April 4 date either. A valuable opportunity to promote McGuigan in the marketing capital of World boxing, New York, was lost.

McGuigan was left with little money yet again, despite the fact that the arrival of Jose Caba, rated somewhere between four and seven in the world, but definitely in the top ten, packed out the King's Hall for the second time.

McGuigan had first decided he could beat Pedroza when he saw the Pedroza-Caba fight on video. Caba had gone fifteen rounds. The fight was decided on points.

Mickey Duff wired the good news home from New York to Eastwood: "Confirming my latest talks with Senior Jose Sulaiman, President of the World Boxing Council, Mexico re Jose Caba versus Barry McGuigan venue King's Hall Ireland championship committee have moved McGuigan to number 10 placing stop. And have further agreed to accept pairing of McGuigan v Caba as an eliminator for World Boxing Council Featherweight championship stop. All rules governing this contest must be agreed by interested parties at a rules meeting to be arranged in Belfast by your commission not later than seven days prior to date of contest."

Before beating Chiteule, McGuigan had been number 14 in the rankings. Caba's fifteen rounds with Pedroza had been scored 5-2 to Pedroza by one judge and 6-2 by another with seven shared. He was going to be tough.

In an effort to recover from the disasters of the Chiteule fight, Eastwood's thoughts turned back to his term in Gleason's Gym. He brought over Bobby McQuillar as coach and Ricky Young and Camello Negron as 1,000 dollar a week sparring partners to help.

McQuillar filled McGuigan with talk about pace, about defence, and about the element of surprise. McQuillar is an addict.

"When they call it the art and the science of self defence they mean exactly that. Art. And science. When you put it together you got the most beautiful thing you ever set eyes upon. Poetry in motion, that's what it is. When you see it done and done right, you're really looking at something.

"I used to think it was against the rules to get hit. So must you."

"We were very much worried about the Chiteule fight," Young Says. "We watched the tapes on television. We thought that he had overworked. He had trained just too hard. So this time we got his weight down early and we pretty much left it to Bobby McQuillar. He's an expert at that — not overworking a guy. Not going past the peak. Once you reach the peak you slow it down.

"Barry was sparring five, six rounds a time for the

Caba fight.

"That fight he proved it. Caba had gone the distance with Pedroza. He proved right then and there that he was ready to step up in class.

"It was a surprise, not that he took out Caba so quickly, but that he handled him with ease. People in America were saying he wasn't ready, that Caba had too much experience for him, and that he wasn't ready for it. He handled him with tremendous ease.

"McGuigan was extremely nervous in the dressing room before the Caba fight. Which is very good.

"They say he gets bad-tempered before a fight," Rick Young says. "But with us he was just so relaxed. The thing that I liked about him was that he wasn't afraid to ask us for advice. Did we think he was doing good or were there many improvements he could make. I respected that. He had the confidence to ask us to tell him certain mistakes that he made and we all pointed our views out. That was good."

McGuigan too was worried: "I wasn't sharp enough. He was catching me. I told people that it would be my hardest fight so far, and I was right. I had to go ten rounds with him and he was so damned awkward. My timing was off and that happens when you are over the top. If I had fought him a week earlier I would have taken him in seven."

McGuigan showed class and strength as he took out Caba in seven. He was back, in Eastwood's resounding phrase "on the bit."

"I was fighting a world class opponent here," McGuigan rapid-fired his assessment of the fight for journalists. "I knew he realised I had a good left hook. He was aware of that left hook and guarded himself very well. He was a very dangerous puncher and when you throw that left hook you leave yourself open. I was told not to work on that until the opportunity arose.

"I deliberately went for the jab and when I realised the jab was working I started sticking them into his chest.

"No he did not hurt me at any stage, oh excuse me, he did hurt me in the second round. I kept my composure and moved back and covered myself well."

The alarm bells of the Chiteule fight were far away. "Every fight you change your tactics. The last fight I didn't have a very good fight and a lot of people were disappointed and I think I was disappointed in a way. I learned something from the last fight and I learned something tonight as well.

"Tonight I had the same old urge in me. I trained hard. Maybe I trained too hard for the last one."

But the significance of the Caba fight was demeaned a little when the visitor got a brief chance to talk to the press. "My manager in Los Angeles," he complained, "he talk to me 128 pound. I come here . . . 126 pounds. I am running maybe two hours and a half this morning. I have sauna. Today I'm tired."

Mickey Duff interjected. "He just got a sweat up this morning that's all. If he had a sauna I didn't see it."

"We had the same problem making the weight for Pedroza," he conceded suddenly. "A year ago he used to make nine stone reasonably comfortably. Now it's 9-2, 9-3."

Duff was pleased that, if American television had not taken this fight, they could now realise how marketable a product McGuigan was. Next time he would have network interest in McGuigan, and the possibility of Big Bucks. There was an idle rumour flying around the bar of the Forum Hotel that Pedroza had promised a voluntary defence of the WBA crown to whoever won between McGuigan and Caba. McGuigan told journalists in his little dressing room that he was not ready. He had still a bit to learn. He preferred to wait.

Caba agreed McGuigan was not ready. "Pedroza has too much intelligence. Maybe fifteen year, maybe twenty year he fight amateur and professional. McGuigan: he young and he strong. But Pedroza too intelligent."

American television was not interested in McGuigan -v- nobody. The European Boxing Union was. They decided that by June 1984, McGuigan had to defend his European title once again. Esteban Eguia, a long time Spanish European contender and a refurbished bantamweight, was nominated.

The spectacle was short-lived. McGuigan appeared to visibly restrain himself. McGuigan took two rounds and forty-five seconds to destroy the Spaniard.

"We could conceivably have lost," Mickey Duff said afterwards. "We could more conceivably have suffered an eye injury." That would have spelt disaster for the financiers of professional boxing who still sought the television deal with American networks and make their fighter more "marketable in the States."

* * * * * * *

9. Breaking Into TV

In keeping with the austere surroundings, the celebrations were reserved. Two great cockneys kept the entire travelling population of Clones out of the dressing room: something that would be unheard of in Belfast, where everybody gets a chance to at least shake McGuigan's hand.

The dressing room inside was like the nave of a cathedral, complete with buttresses at the corner. There was not much to say: blame the European Boxing Union for putting poor Eguia up, thank the manager and trainer and family and people of London. This was getting to be a bit of a routine.

But another milestone had been passed — McGuigan had topped the bill in the Royal Albert Hall at twenty-three years of age. It was a nice thought as his taxi brought him back around the edges of Hyde Park to the Holiday Inn.

The Albert Hall always seems a slightly incongruous venue for boxing. It stood a bulwark of pomposity as thousands of working-class folk filled its seats.

The audience was addressed as "My Lords and Ladies" by the MC. They also introduced McGuigan as "Featherweight champion of Great Britain."

The British fans who came were there "to see McGuigan". So far they had read about him in *Boxing News* and seen him on television. No matter what the hype was, he was an exciting boxer.

Even the relatively straightforward task of warning the boxing fans not to buy their tickets on the black market was turned into a lecture from an invisible headmaster... "We are urging you in your own interest not to buy tickets from touts. These unauthorised tickets being touted outside the hall are not valid for sale. They are clearly marked as such too. Since this obnoxious nuisance shows no signs of diminishing — quite the opposite in fact — we must warn you that anyone seen purchasing such tickets is liable to be refused admission."

Marketing strategy was to be a dominant theme of McGuigan's performances in 1984. In the Albert Hall, the blue flag made its debut.

Duff felt that this was a time to play up the British aspect of McGuigan's split heritage. Eastwood said no. He produced a blue flag with a dove (in the Monaghan county GAA colours) and said that McGuigan would enter the ring behind it. "We're trying to sell him as British," Duff said. Eastwood won, as usual.

The Rocky theme music had run its course while all this was happening, and they had to start the tape again. But the blue flag was one of the most successful ploys in the marketing of McGuigan the peacemaker. As always, it had a strong commercial flavour. The flag was modelled on the flag of the Holiday Inn, where the party were staying.

Eastwood said it was unlikely McGuigan would fight in London again, "although they had been treated well." The British papers had played up the peacemaker image all week. They came to Eastwood on the morning after the fight looking for news of the next big contest. And met the religious problems in Northern Ireland staring them in the face.

A fight against Paul de Vorce, easily the most difficult opponent McGuigan had faced, had been agreed. The problem was the timing and venue. The best time for American television would be a Sunday, but Sunday in Belfast would offend religious groups. The other options were Dublin where the only realistic venue, the RDS, would prove too expensive, or England. There was also the option of staging it at midnight, so the fight would actually occur on Monday morning. The difficulty sounded absurd. Absurd but newsworthy.

McGuigan's 1984 campaign was nothing if not newsworthy.

The fight would probably have gone to Navan, after a check by the Eastwoods found it was available. In fact the solution was found almost immediately, on June 12, because CBS had to change days. Saturday afternoon (US time) would be time enough for McGuigan's American television appearance. The fight could go ahead on Saturday night without too much trouble. It came within three weeks of the European title defence in London, which relegated the Eguia scrap to something akin to a sparring session. McGuigan had to delay his Caribbean holiday for this fight.

CBS had two free dates in July to offer. Neither proved suitable. A last minute reshuffle of their programming gave McGuigan his big break. A large CBS sign was hoisted over the ring at the King's Hall. McGuigan was going to America after all.

The fight was a screen test. The opponent was a tight boxer who could undo McGuigan. He was a three times Golden Gloves champion as an amateur, was never on the deck as an amateur or a professional, and was on the way up, in contrast to the way-back-down fighters like Caba and Chiteule.

McGuigan had to work very hard on his style for the De Vorce fight.

* * * * * * *

10. The Amachewer

It was very important to beat De Vorce. It involved a certain style, McGuigan committing himself to a certain style and staying with that commitment. He could decide to counter-punch him, to move and box, or else be aggressive, buzz and buzz and buzz, and come forward throwing shots.

Even if the style McGuigan had decided on was not working, he was advised to keep with it. To change would be fatal. Do one type of thing, do it often. That was the way to beat De Vorce.

The hope was that after the first few rounds, McGuigan's consistent attack would get to De Vorce. The idea was to demoralise the American. Then batter him.

The De Vorce corner were not demoralised, but their fighter was taking a hammering from the start: "He's got nothing for chrissake. He's an amachewer." After a minute and fifty seconds of the fifth round, McGuigan was not only the victor, but victor in the most professional manner conceivable.

The crowd were hyped up to even higher levels than they previously experienced because of the ten minute delay between the previous support bout and the main attraction. The whole point of the exercise was American television. So the crowd waited for American television.

There was nothing to do except chant, then sing, then applaud. One side against the other. Trying to outshout each other. Then chant. Then sing. Then applaud.

That did not mean that the voices were spent before the fighting had started. McGuigan's regal entry into the King's Hall, the starter's flag and the chase around the ring, McGuigan, in manager-Eastwood's phrase constantly "on the bit."

Every one of the five rounds went to McGuigan. The pace never relented: two rights to the head in the first, two fine rib crushing lefts in the second, a powerful left jab in the third, and more body shots in the fourth.

McGuigan was scoring, scoring, scoring. And when the two went into a crouch in the fifth, he snapped one around the corner, high into De Vorce's unsupported ribs.

De Vorce had expected an uppercut and opened a gap under his shoulder. The ribs bent in and sprung out again with the force of the blow. Syd Nathan, the referee, heard a low moan and decided immediately that De Vorce had been winded. There was nothing left. The crowd chanted with delight, but later mourned into their pints that they thought it was a bad decision.

Some said the decision was premature. Referee Nathan countered: "You don't just stop a fight when a boxer goes down. He was prepared to stay up there and take much more punishment. He had taken too much already."

Bill Sheerin of the British Boxing Board of Control asked "What do these people want, a coffin? We are constantly being abused by the medical people about boxing. The referee's job is to protect the guy who's getting beaten. If somebody is losing and likely to get hurt the fight gets stopped. Do people think that if they pay their money they are entitled to a full ten rounds whatever the consequence? Do they want it to go on until somebody is badly hurt?"

* * * * * * *

11. Orozco

In the McGuigan dressing room three important names were being mentioned. The TV screen test was a success, so now there was probably half a million dollars available to tempt Eusebio Pedroza to Belfast.

The name of Pedroza was becoming a household name in Ireland, among people who had never heard of the Panamanian twelve months beforehand. Wilfred Gomez, the WBC champion was also mentioned as a possible opponent. So was Rocky Lockridge, the junior lightweight WBA champion. Later Gomez was to lose his title and take Lockridge's.

But for prestige, the Eastwoods wanted Pedroza.

As for McGuigan, he would be happy to get two more fights before taking on any champion. He was right, in a sort of a way. The price of Pedroza, £250,000 worth of conditions on top of his purse, and the fact that Gomez had another fight on hand made Lockridge a possibility. But the Belfast public were tired of speculation. They wanted some hard news.

The television deal was an outstanding success. McGuigan, unlike many of the modern-day TV boxers in America, had been discovered by television, not made by television. His two last King's Hall fights before the World title, against Felipe Orozco and Juan Laporte, were to confirm the television interest in McGuigan.

The opponent was to have been Angel Mayor, from Venezuela. Mayor failed to appear. Two days before the fight, Eastwood told him not to bother. "Tomorrow he come," his manager said. "Forget it," said Eastwood.

Duff's contacts in New York began to suspect something was wrong early in the week. There was a World Boxing Council convention in Panama which would involve a lot of gossip about this new Irishman that was challenging the Latin American and United States power base in the featherweight division.

The barons of boxing were upset about a Belfast promoter getting in on their scene so successfully. Mayor was under pressure not to travel. His late withdrawal would mean that Duff's and Eastwood's credibility with the American television companies would be damaged. Mayor could be compensated with fights in Atlantic City and Las Vegas.

Realising what was about to happen Duff was already looking for a replacement. Felipe Orozco was preparing for another contest. He was pulled over to Belfast. The fight went ahead. NBC were satisfied. McGuigan and his sparring partners now had to prepare themselves to face a southpaw at short notice.

Hughie Russell, in Eastwood's stable, was a southpaw, but he never sparred with McGuigan. Rick Young regards this as the most testing time in which he trained with McGuigan.

The withdrawal of Mayor was a blow to the Eastwood image in Belfast. The sceptics began to doubt the authenticity of the whole performance. One correspondent to the *Irish News* in Belfast wrote:

"We have had the lot. Six 'twos', four 'threes' — what next, a Yankee? Boxers are not turning up. Boxers are retiring to accommodate TV fights stopped for no other reason than one was scowling at the other. Poor match-making. Undue delays between fights, and finally, the ultimate, Minter on Saturday night.

"We are mad about boxing and Barry, but we are not that far gone to continue to support such sham shows infinitum. The Eastwood clan have abused the generosity of boxing fans here once again."

Eastwood too was doubting the credibility of some of the forces that run world boxing.

The fight that eventually did get under way was against Felipe Orozco. Beanpole they called him. Other than his extraordinary height and the fact he was a southpaw not much was known about him. Eddie Shaw mourned about the preparation that had been done on Angel Mayor, and the fact that so little was known about Orozco.

Orozco came from Colombia. He was a junior featherweight, four pounds lighter than featherweight, and had just reached the peak of his career, fifth in the WBC rankings, fifth in the *Ring* magazine rankings, third in the International Boxing Writers rankings, and tenth in the WBA rankings. But he was growing too heavy for that division.

But these credentials meant nothing. In the eyes of the Belfast public he was a substitute. "I hate substitutes, and I hate southpaws," Barney Eastwood thundered in the Saturday morning newspapers. The crowds had more faith in McGuigan than to ignore another vital fight before the television cameras.

This time NBC took the fight to American viewers. The major change they effected was the removal of Smirnoff's name from the corner pads of the ring in favour of W&A Gilbey. Not that many people had time to notice the name on the corner pads anyway. The fight was over in the second round. American viewers dawdling through the various television stations scarcely had time for a hamburger.

Two minutes and ten seconds into the second round McGuigan caught Orozco with about six punches, culminating in a right to the body and a left to the head.

The after-fight interviews for American television lasted longer than the fight itself.

McGuigan had never fought a southpaw in his career. He cautiously worked his way into the first round moving forward all the time, getting caught by Orozco twice, but soon adapting to meet the tall southpaw. As a body-puncher, a fight against Orozco simply meant there was more body to aim at.

"One of the punches I caught him with sent a tingle back up to my elbow," McGuigan said. "When you feel a tingle like that you know he's hurt."

He still talked about two fights before meeting the champion. Again he was right in a sort of a way. He was to have one more real fight, against Juan Laporte and two half ones.

* * * * * * *

12. "Leave the fighting to McGuigan . . ."

When McGuigan became British champion his politics became an issue. McGuigan's family is quite political. His uncle was a Sinn Fein councillor in the 1950s and there is a tradition of allegiance to republican Fianna Fail in the family. But in recent years economics has overtaken the border as the dominant issue in Republic of Ireland politics and McGuigan showed no political preferences of his own. He is a pacifist and always told anyone who asked him that he did not concern himself with Northern Ireland politics.

Anyway, boxing tended to draw support from both the Nationalist-Catholic and Unionist-Protestant areas of Belfast. The British press began to see opportunities for news feature material.

And when McGuigan became European champion the features gained even more prominence. On September 25 1983 the Manchester-based *Daily Mirror* sportswriter, Ted Macauley, ran a feature on McGuigan: "the fighter who makes EVERYONE forget."

". . . . The rivals by knocking them out, the fans by making them happy. McGuigan with Northern Irish parents but born in the South, has dual nationality and is careful to wear neutral colours — no greens, no oranges — when he steps into the ring."

For the first time many of the now-familiar McGuigan quotes began to appear: "I don't care what colour, nationality or religion anybody is, I'm in the business of fighting and making a living. And if I can unite people and make them happy, then I'm happy.

"When they're cheering me they forget everything else. All their troubles and differences are gone. It's my side they're on.

"In Belfast they have an expression: Leave the fighting to McGuigan."

The quotes got bolder as time went on. They inspired enthusiasm in visiting journalists.

On November 29 1983 the *Daily Express* joined in with Barry "leading the fight for a united Ulster."

"This is a picture of Belfast that all Northern Ireland has been waiting to see . . ."

A picture above the text showed a smiling McGuigan with all his friends and accomplices posed behind.

"The Falls and the Shankill in the same ring — but on the same side . . ."

The next picture showed "Barry (a Catholic) with his (Protestant) wife Sandra."

Barry was quoted: "People who were divided in many other things have really started coming together to share Northern Ireland boxing successes. And that means more to me than winning titles."

Eastwood echoed McGuigan's anthem: "anyone who was at the King's Hall would have wondered why we were divided. We need to be united on something and I think Barry has brought back our old pride and unity."

George Kimball, one of America's best known boxing writers — he writes for the *Boston Globe* — wrote in *Ring* magazine in December 1984: "In a country where people can sit in a pub and argue about whether or not it is raining outside (those espousing the former position would usually be right) there is unanimity over at least one subject. Diehard Unionists from the city's hard-line Shankill

Road district sit side-by-side with fervent Republicans from the South cheering McGuigan with a singleminded devotion. The ancient animosities are laid to rest, and those representing both sides of the Irish question close ranks behind him."

Hugh McIlvanney, the award-winning British sportswriter wrote in the *Observer*, a London Sunday newspaper: "In Ireland where one man's hero can be the next man's villain, the emotional identification with this remarkable twenty-three year-old is so deep and so close to being unanimous that it sends an awed shudder through a witness from outside the island. McGuigan's status as an All-Ireland hero relates on one hand to the powerful and persistent hunger for such a phenomenon and on the other to the considerable charm of his personality and the exciting dimensions of his talent."

But supporting Barry McGuigan was an easy concession to unity. It did not cost money. It did not involve any concession of principle. Like going to the theatre or backing a horse, sport falls well outside the realm of divided Ulster. Most of the time, anyway.

Sport in Northern Ireland has survived seventeen years of troubled times. Sectarian violence on the football terraces there is nothing new. The staunchly Protestant soccer club, Linfield and its Catholic counterpoint Belfast Celtic, were the first to suffer from the symptoms of inter-religious violence. The two matches generally regarded as being the touchstones of this violent tradition happened in 1912 and 1948. In 1912 a revolver was fired in the air at a match between the clubs and fighting broke out on the terraces. In 1948, a stormy match between the clubs finished in four players being sent to the line for violent play, numerous crowd invasions of the field, and a Celtic player, Jimmy Jones, having his leg broken by a Loyalist mob after the game.

In latter years the violence continued. In 1970 Derry City, the team from the Roman Catholic enclave of the same name, was expelled from the Irish League because visiting clubs refused to play at its home ground. In 1979, Linfield supporters rioted and left a trail of destruction through Dundalk, a town just across the border in the Irish Republic, and several matches between Linfield and a club newly adopted by Catholic supporters, Cliftonvllle, resulted in riots. Linfield subsequently refused to play on Cliftonville's ground.

Gaelic football is almost exclusively played by members of the Nationalist Roman Catholic community in Northern Ireland. On one occasion, broken glass was scattered over a field in Tyrone to prevent a Gaelic match being played and Gaelic club centres were frequently firebombed.

But most sports succeeded in remaining aloof from the turmoil. Basketball, a new sport in Belfast, prides itself on its peaceful image and the fact that it draws support from both sides of the community.

And despite the inter-club tensions, when the Northern Ireland soccer team qualified for the semi-final groupings (the last eight) of the 1982 World Cup, they drew their support from both Nationalists and Unionists. Ironically, members of the team from opposite sides of the divide even had brothers in jail for terrorist offences against each other.

But the situation is not clear-cut. While support for the Irish rugby team broke down barriers, sports like hockey and cricket were regarded as almost exclusively Unionist.

But boxing was never divided. Clubs like Holy Family, Sacred Heart, Holy Trinity, Oliver Plunkett, Immaculata, Star, St Georges, and RUC boxed each other. The walls of the Workingman's Club in the Unionist Shankill district are decorated with pictures of the Queen alongside boxers who came from Nationalist areas like Rinty Monaghan, John Caldwell and Freddy Gilroy.

At the height of the troubles in the early 1970s the cars outside the Holy Family boxing club on the Falls were left untouched while all other cars in the area were being burned.

When the Eastwood boxing circus revived the professional tradition in Northern Ireland, the old boxing fans re-emerged to experience again the remembered joys of the fifties and early sixties. They brought their younger friends and relatives with them. Somebody, somewhere, was bound to point and say "look, Catholics and Protestants that are not fighting each other."

The Eastwoods vigorously maintain that the peace image was not promoted by them at any stage. But soon the slogans started emerging for foreign living-room consumption: "Barry is the only man who can walk down the Falls and the Shankill and be as welcome in both of them" . . . "leave the fighting to McGuigan, they say in Belfast" . . . and the irony of a man pursuing peace through a career in the most violent of sports began to attract media attention.

* * * * * * *

13. "Try not to be a wally . . ."

Once the issue was raised it would not go away. The litany of bridges that McGuigan was building was retold: the young man from just south of the border, moving just north of the border within a mile of Clones. His marrying his Protestant childhood sweetheart from across the road. His moving to Belfast and taking up British citizenship to fight for the British title. Eventually the flag of peace, a rejection of the tricolour and Union Jack, and use of local folk air "Danny Boy" as a substitute national anthem.

The outside view was summed up by Richard Ford of *The Times* of London: "Orange or green, tricolour or Union flag? It makes little difference to the Irish when they are applauding a home-grown champion. As one British minister said while watching Catholics and Protestants cheering deliriously together after a McGuigan victory: 'Whatever that boy has got to bring them together, I wish I had it'."

One step wrong and McGuigan will find himself isolated. If McGuigan fought an opponent from the Shankill for the British title, in the same way as Hugh Russell and Dave Larmour fought for the British Bantamweight title, his support would be momentarily divided. But it would cement again just as it did for both Russell and Larmour when they next fought other opponents.

McGuigan's stance is dangerous because it could be seen

to trivialise the problem, to draw attention to it unnecessarily in a sporting context, or to come down on the side of one interpretation of the Northern Ireland problem. That the problem is one of Protestants and Catholics fighting each other, not one of Nationalists and Unionists fighting external influences.

When McGuigan was accepting a sportstar of the year award early in 1984 he told the assembled guests "My first wish for 1984 is for peace in Northern Ireland. I think you can guess the second."

McGuigan approached the peacemaker image with his usual innocent enthusiasm. In 1981, when he was asked about the fact that Protestants were supporting his fights despite the fact he was a Free Stater, he speculated at the impact "somebody famous" could have by giving an ecumenical example to the working class people caught up in the troubles.

The difficulty was to hold the line in the face of the efforts of the Fleet Street tabloids. In the words of *The Daily Mail*, it was "McGuigan the good bringing pride to a troubled land."

Tom McGurk, a journalist from Tyrone, Northern Ireland, said in the Dublin-based *Sunday Independent* after the World title fight: "Soon the Belfast Forum hotel was stuffed with the Fleet Street hacks doing what their editors called 'The most positive story to come out of Northern Ireland since the Peace people.' The fact that now, when according to Fleet Street all Northern Ireland is united behind Barry, while in fact they seem to be following his pugilistic example in the local council chambers, is irrelevant. As always with the tabloid men from Fleet Street — never allow the facts to interfere with a good story. Another B.J. Eastwood winner."

And of course the peacemaker questions arose even at the World championship press conference. McGuigan fielded them neatly. "I have always said I was for peace and harmony. What else could I be in favour of? I hope my boxing has made people in Ireland more friendly to each other."

Somebody asked if he was interested in going into politics!

The peacemaker image almost took a standing eight-count when the first instalments of the exclusive £50,000 Barry McGuigan story in the *Daily Star* appeared the week before the World title fight.

McGuigan was quoted as saying: "I used to cycle nine miles through IRA terrorist country to Wattlebridge. My mother used to be terrified that something would happen to me.

"One night two men were found murdered by the IRA in a hedge on my route to the club. They had been pitchforked to death.

"My mother wanted me to quit, but my father persuaded her that as these were sectarian killings I, as an innocent lad, was in no danger.

"Since those days he has never wanted me to do anything except box. Boxing became like a drug. I couldn't have given it up. It holds something for me that I cannot explain. I'm not the sort of bloke who likes hitting people. I'm not violent or aggressive. I don't want to conquer the world — except as a boxer."

It is likely that the words "by the IRA" were added by the *Daily Star* writers as they ghosted the McGuigan article. Michael Naan and Andrew Murray had been murdered by members of the Argyle and Sutherland Highlanders, a British Army regiment serving in the area, who were later convicted of murder. The murders were a highly emotive incident at the height of the troubles in the area.

Callers to the McGuigan household on the day that the article appeared included the distraught mother of one of the victims. Pat McGuigan denied that Barry would have said anything like that when questioned by Dublin newspapers.

Sinn Fein party members condemned the statement. The chairman of Fermanagh District Council, Paul Corrigan, described the article as "one of the most obnoxious ever published against the oppressed people in South Fermanagh especially the reference to the pitchfork murder carried out by the British army."

But Sinn Fein, the extreme Republican Party, seemed to hold no objection to McGuigan taking up British citizenship or fighting for the British title.

Meanwhile, that window on extreme opinion in Northern Ireland, the graffiti walls declared: *Barry the Brit sells his soul for English Gold.*

An Phoblacht also published an article from their sports correspondent in January 1985 on McGuigan: "As an explosive hard-hitting boxer there is nobody as exciting to watch in the sport today and the fact that he is an Irishman makes that all the more satisfying.

"Now I don't give a damn about whether a British passport is not as Republican as a Free State's one with a harp on the front, or a blue EEC one, or whether it is possible to box your way to the top from a non-existent Irish professional scene, or whether you have to go to the United States — abandoning Irish citizenship for American citizenship is apparently not a crime to the green purists who understand such niceties.

"But all the boring nonsense aside, what I am finding increasingly objectionable about Barry is that the Clones Cyclone is turning into a proper little wimp. More and more he is allowing his handlers to portray him as a '*symbol of unity across the divide*' and coming out with ridiculous platitudes which the British just adore.

"Not since Ciaran McKeown and the Peace women have we had such unadulterated saccharine bullshit as these empty phrases about uniting the Falls and the Shankill on the night of Barry's fights.

"Are the paid perjury victims released to watch your fights, Barry? Do the crown forces stop harassment on the streets during your fights? Is there no strip-searching in Armagh when you are stripping off for the weigh-in, Barry?

"If you want to get involved in politics then get involved, but don't make an idiot of yourself with rose-petal platitudes about peace which only insult your supporters. Address yourself to the whole question or to none of it.

"Let's face it, preaching and goodwill does not sit too well on a guy who makes his living knocking the hell out of his opponents for money. How many boxers end up punch-drunk imbeciles? How many die at an early age?

"And to be brutally frank, Barry McGuigan, prizefighter for peace, has already killed one opponent on his way to glory, and it didn't stop him hitting as hard as ever since then. And that was for money, not for a cause.

"That's what the boxing game is all about. It's brutal, but I don't claim to be a pacifist, so it's fine by me.

"One word of advice, Barry old son. We're all rooting for you in the ring, but try not to be a wally out of it, it's so disappointing and not a little insulting. You can bring a world title to Clones without becoming a British propaganda stooge."

At one level, McGuigan's cross-the-divide stance seemed to work. When McGuigan was given a civic reception in Belfast City Hall, councillor George Seawright was among the first to congratulate him. Seawright had previously received a prison sentence for a remark that "Roman Catholics should be incinerated."

Immediately after McGuigan won the World title, in the chamber of the Northern Ireland Assembly, Seamus Close, a Roman Catholic Unionist with the moderate Alliance Party, described McGuigan as a hero. The leader of the extremist Unionist party, the Democratic Unionist Party, interjected. "We have heroes in the RUC."

Close continued that McGuigan was a man of peace and reconciliation and he hoped the members of the Assembly would follow his example. "At the fight people embraced each other. There was no violence, no distraction."

Another DUP interjection, this time from Rev Ivan Foster, came: "Fifteen rounds of it."

Paisley also raised the ire of nationalists by referring to McGuigan as the British boxer who had lifted the World crown.

The politics continued unabated.

When McGuigan was considering turning professional in 1980, there was not even an Irish Boxing Board of Control. The previous tradition was for Ireland to affiliate as an area of the British Boxing Board of Control. Irish professional boxers who wanted to get anywhere fought for British titles.

And a fair array of them had. Cork-born Jack Doyle

fought for the British Heavyweight title in 1933, Cork-born Mick Leahy held the British Middleweight title from 1963 to 1964, Dublin-born Pat McCormack held the British light-welterweight title during 1974 and John McCormack held the British light-heavyweight title from 1967 to 1969. When Charlie Nash fought for the World title in 1980, he entered the ring behind a tricolour. Nash, another British title holder, is from Derry, in Northern Ireland.

Most of these boxers were based outside Ireland. McGuigan had the added advantage of being based at home. He moved to Belfast before fights. The rest of the time he lived in Clones. Home was not clearly defined. Seeking the British title in the circumstances was controversial.

Because he continued to live in Clones, McGuigan feared objections from boxing people who would regard him as ineligible for the British title. Hence the British citizenship.

As it turned out, holding a British passport was not necessary. He could have remained a Republic of Ireland citizen and fought as British champion. He also qualified as Irish featherweight champion when a controlling professional body was eventually set up in Dublin, Aontacht Dornálaíocht na hÉireann, the Boxing Union of Ireland, run by Joe Christle, father of one of the premier Irish boxing families of the late 1970s and by barrister Seamus O Tuathail.

To become Irish champion is not exactly difficult. There are only a dozen or so boxers based in Ireland. The BUI controls promotions in the Republic of Ireland, boxers from anywhere in the thirty-two counties are entitled to hold its titles, but it is toothless. It took no action for instance when its directives regarding a promotion in Cork were ignored.

McGuigan took the opportunity to climb through the European ranks. Being British title holder is a respected position in the eyes of the European Boxing Union. As soon as McGuigan had won the British title he automatically progressed to the European championship. Britain usually has two or three boxers in the top ten of each division.

The only other acceptable path to the top was to operate from America. This route was chosen by light-middleweight Sean Mannion, from Galway, who operates from Jim Connolly's gym in Boston and fought Mike McCallum for the WBC World light-middleweight title in October 1984.

McGuigan, as a registered British citizen, now pays taxes in Northern Ireland. Taxation is less severe in Northern Ireland than in the South. His house is within fifty yards of the border, on the Northern side.

He takes his electricity from the south, his water and telephone from the north. A small terminal for the electricity near the house is on the southern side of the border. On his favourite three mile circuit of roads near his house he crosses and recrosses the border several times.

The issue of whether he is British or Irish created so much controversy in early 1985 that an RTE radio programme, *The Gay Byrne Hour*, contacted Pat McGuigan. Does Barry fight for Ireland or Britain? McGuigan pondered. "Amateurs fight for their countries. Professionals fight for money."

* * * * * * *

14. The Ghost

When McGuigan fought Eguila in the Albert Hall in June, Clyde Ruan emerged as the top contender for the British featherweight crown. It had been eighteen months since McGuigan had won the title. Ruan wanted a defence. He reckoned, that with a little work from Charm Chiteule and by exploiting McGuigan's weaknesses, he could take McGuigan's British and European titles from him.

The normal practice was for boxers who went in search of World titles to relinquish the mere British and European crowns that they had once held. Pat Cowdell had opened the way for McGuigan to win the vacant British featherweight title in this fashion. Loris Stecca had left the way clear for McGuigan to win the European title. McGuigan resolved from the moment that he won both titles that he would defend them.

It was back to the 2,500 seat auditorium of the Ulster Hall to defend against Clyde Ruan. Ruan was lucky to be there — he had been confused when he was given the verdict against Pat Doherty in a final eliminator for the British title, on the flat of his back on the canvas, victim of an illegal blow that had been thrown after the final bell had sounded.

The odds of eight to one on were justified. The average knock-out distance of four rounds was maintained. McGuigan spoke afterwards of "showing the public what I was capable of and what they had come to see."

He had settled in and enjoyed himself, and admitted almost apologetically that he waited for the fourth round signal that would let him end the fight.

Then it was back to the unrestful relief of the dressing room. "Orchestra only" a notice stuck with sticking plaster on the wall said. McGuigan gave his solo performance with studied comments, careful not to sound cocky, or gloating.

There had been worries. McGuigan had been too light in the weeks leading up to the fight. He had taken three days off training to increase his weight somewhat.

Ruan arrived to publicly congratulate McGuigan. For public consumption he was "glad to be beaten by the future World champion." McGuigan was told to get dressed before he got cold by Eastwood. He insisted on carrying on with his umpteenth interview for the umpteenth pressman. "Sign one for the referee, the referee wants a signed poster," somebody cried from the back of the bunch.

McGuigan turned away from the swarm. He lifted his underpants, facing the wall in a desperate effort at modesty in his moment of triumph. Quick change, a blink of his tired eyes, and he turned around to face the crowd. "Right," he said. "Who wants this photograph taken?"

The Ulster Hall, he felt, was less noisy, more intimate. It was probably the last appearance there.

He had banished the ghost of the illfated Charm Chiteule fight the previous January. Chiteule had coached Ruan on how to get at McGuigan, how to cope. Ruan coped with the left hook. But he said "this man moves so well. It's not his punching that makes McGuigan so different, it's that he moves so damn well."

Some journalist had a bright idea. "Is he a ghost?" he asked.

"Yeah he's forever working."

"Would you describe him as a ghost? You know, there one minute, gone the next."

"Yeah."

"McGuigan is the ghost," said Ruan. The teleprinters rattled in Britain.

For McGuigan it was like doing Chiteule over again, perfectly this time. He saw in the third that Ruan was spent. He was told to go in in the fourth round. When he got in at close range he caused immense trouble. Then came a burst of punches, a short left hook, another left hook, Ruan was down, the crowd were on their feet in a frenzy, and anybody who had laid £8 on a McGuigan victory could happily collect his 20p winnings after tax.

Ruan had been easily beaten, but McGuigan says that he has to train to suit each individual opponent. "Once there is someone in the other corner trying to knock your block off, it doesn't matter who they are, you don't have any problem psyching yourself up."

A month later, McGuigan was psyching up for the last major obstacle in his path to the World championship.

Perspiration flies through the charged air of the King's Hall, McGuigan's defeat of Juan Laporte opened the way for a crack at the World title.

Family man: Barry's wife Sandra, son Blaine and thumbs up from a champion.

CHAPTER 6

Chasing A Champion

"Money doesn't grow on trees. I should know that better than anyone."
— Barney Eastwood on the cost of staging a World title fight.

1. Laporte In Ten

The victims were hardly household names . . . Nati . . . Chiteule . . . Caba . . . De Vorce . . . Orozco. Juan Laporte was a household name. His name carried authority on the NBC Saturday afternoon television schedule. He was not a World Champion. But he might have been.

At twenty-five, Laporte was young for an ex-champion. He had taken the vacant World Boxing Council title after Salvador Sanchez had died in a car crash. Then he broke a thumb in a defence against Wilfredo Gomez. And lost the title.

The marketing of Laporte was as a street-wise guy, a poor boy from the tough Bedford-Stuyvesant area, a Puerto Rican ghetto in New York. He was spotted by old pro, Carlos Espada, when he was in danger of becoming a professional car thief. He became Puerto Rican bantamweight champion in 1976 at the age of sixteen (the same age as McGuigan when he won the Ulster senior title), and New York Golden Gloves winner. A professional at seventeen, after an amateur career of thirty-five matches and twenty-nine wins, signing the contract just a month before his eighteenth birthday.

At twenty he fought for the NBC featherweight title

held by Salvador Sanchez and lost. At twenty-one he fought for the WBA junior lightweight title and lost. At twenty-two he fought for the WBA featherweight title and lost against Pedroza. At twenty-three he won the vacant WBC featherweight title. At twenty-four he lost it again. At twenty-five he met McGuigan, when he was a year older than the Irishman, just four fights more on the record, but with overpowering experience and status in world featherweight boxing . . . fourth in the world according to *Ring* magazine, behind Pedroza, Nelson and Gomez.

Laporte thought he was unlucky, so he gambled on an even more prestigious title, that nominated by the World Boxing Association and held by Eusebio Pedroza. Laporte fought Pedroza in the gambling centre of Atlantic City on January 24, 1982 and lost one of the most controversial fights of modern featherweight history.

Pedroza won over fifteen rounds, but Laporte was hailed as the victim of a piece of dirty work . . . low punches, kidney punches, elbows, everything that could be found outside the rulebook. It was a fight that stained Pedroza's already sinister reputation.

Referee Gay Jutras took two points from Pedroza for repeated fouling. Laporte's manager, Howie Albert, sent a videotape to the WBA with a catalogue of crimes — fourteen low blows, twenty-five kidney punches and fifty-eight fouls in all. The WBA are used to complaints and sent the video back.

The fight was close until round twelve, then Laporte fell away, reportedly hurt by the fouls. "I won't say his fouling beat me," Laporte said, "because I don't think I lost."

The New Jersey State commission reversed the decision. The WBA held firm. Pedroza just said, "real men don't cry or make excuses." But what was done or said did not really matter. What mattered was that Laporte was in the Pedroza class, and McGuigan's aspirations would depend on beating Laporte.

The Laporte fight was a triumph for Eastwood's marketing skills. For over a year McGuigan fights had come to dominate social life in the city. Crowds like he attracted were not regarded as part of boxing anymore. They were, like full length togs and newsreel films, part of another age. Yet the February 23 date with Laporte was the fifth time McGuigan filled 7,000 seats in Belfast's King's Hall. This time the tickets were sold three weeks in advance. This time people stood at the back of the seating against the wall, climbed on hoardings and stood wherever they might get a glimpse of a low flying left hook to the body. The tradition of the 1930s was back.

A year beforehand the name of Juan Laporte might not have been as familiar to the Belfast fans. They were betting on McGuigan at 5/2 on. Anywhere else Laporte should be favourite.

The Eastwood formula was to provide the hype: the picture of a grinning boxer with a globe "Barry McGuigan with the whole world in his hands"; the "was it on-was it off" debate about live television; the daily reports that all was well in training and Barry McGuigan was exuding his normal cocky-cautious optimism. Cautious it was. No Chiteule style mistakes. This time he sparred for forty rounds.

Although Laporte was not a World Champion, he might have been. He was one of the twenty fighters who have held one or other of the two main World Featherweight titles since 1970. He was only twenty-five. He had fought Sanchez for the WBC title when McGuigan was still recovering from the Olympics in December 1980. He had lost to Pedroza when McGuigan was still at the Luis de la Sagra stage. He was experienced, yet he was less than two years older than McGuigan. On the night of the fight it looked more like ten.

McGuigan won impressively, clocking up the points with his two-fisted marauding for all ten rounds. Laporte defended. Defended and lured. "He has put men away with that single right-hander," McGuigan said. "I proved a few difficult things to myself tonight." The first was that McGuigan could take a punch. In fact he could take two punches.

In the fifth round McGuigan had built up a comfortable lead when two short rights slammed into his face in quick succession. McGuigan staggered backwards. His head was snapped back by another right. The King's Hall was thrown into shock. Danger lights appeared in 7,000 eyes. McGuigan's legs began to draw apart and he grasped his opponent and held him for a second.

The referee stepped in, but the balance was back. McGuigan stayed, even fought back for the rest of the round. There had been a full minute to go when Laporte struck.

Despite the set-back McGuigan extended his lead. The fight continued on its merry McGuigan incline, and the crowd roared on. Until the ninth. This time when the right thundered into McGuigan's jaw, it scarcely had an impact. "I can take a punch and recover," McGuigan repeated. "I can go ten rounds like that."

Laporte had never been knocked down. He came close to it in the final minute when McGuigan zapped punch after punch to the opponent's head as the crowd danced on their chairs. The referee, Harry Gibbs, awarded the fight immediately to McGuigan — he scored the fight 99-97 (6-2-2 in rounds).

2. Contender

After he beat Laporte, people talked about logic. The only logical challenger for the World featherweight title, Barry McGuigan. "How do you think it looked for TV?" McGuigan asked, sitting on his table in the upstairs dressing room (the old downstairs one of Nati days had long since been vacated).

"Laporte wanted it to be sportsmanlike. We agreed there would be no animosity in the build-up. Just to prove that professional fighters can be gentlemanly. There is no need for bitterness."

It was the triumph of the left hook to the body, knocking the strength from Laporte again and again at a rate of thirty punches a minute, for half an hour not counting the breaks. Laporte watched for the break to unleash the right, threw an odd uppercut, stood and counterpunched when he needed to, and was patient.

In the dressing room Laporte's patience ran out. "I've had it," he said. "I promised myself that as soon as I was knocked out or hurt during a fight I would retire. I was hurt tonight." Manager Howie Albert shrugged his shoulders. "But tomorrow, Juan?" Albert said. "I will feel the same way tomorrow," Laporte replied slowly. And he did.

"He was a good fighter and good fighters seem to bring out the best in me," McGuigan said. "I was told to keep pressurising him and that is what I did. It's always worrying to know if you can take a shot. I did, and came back at him."

Ring magazine accredited McGuigan with their Fighter of the Month selection on the basis of that performance, and reported: "McGuigan is a throw-back to the old style of fighting. He comes forward, bobbing and weaving, gloves held high, and, having made an opening, is not content to jab and move away. He stands his ground and having got within range punches away hard and accurately."

After all the excitement there were doubts. Laporte was in decline. At the end of 1983 he had lost a non-title ten rounder to Gerald Hayes, then lost the WBC title to Wilfredo Gomez in twelve rounds. He also needed a points verdict to beat the unrated Dwight Pratchett in his second and last fight of 1984. That was bad news for a hard hitter.

* * * * * * *

3. Reaction

Suddenly, unbelievably simply, all the routes were opened for Barry McGuigan. Ten rounds of quick fire action, about 100 punches a round, those that sat on front of the video recording and counted declared, had bombarded the sensibilities of every boxing manager, promoter, fan, matchmaker, analyst or journalist. The slog and the trekking to the doors of ABC American network companies with the story, "I've got a fighter you might be interested in, he's hot," was over.

The American reaction surpassed even the Eastwoods'

wildest dreams. McGuigan was sold. In one fight. It need not have been so. McGuigan's big fight coincided with a freak heat wave that drove thousands of Americans to the beaches and parks. Only eight million stayed at home to watch the fight. Those that did had a treat.

The television relay was done by **CBS**. Associate director of sports, Rick Gentile, was ecstatic about the reaction to the fight. Not that the viewing figure of eight million was high. But on a freakishly hot afternoon when thousands of East Coast residents took to the country he regarded it as a good reaction. Gentile was even more excited about the venue. Belfast was comparable to fights by Billy Costello (whose brother Vinnie had sparred with Barry in New York) in Kingston, upstate New York.

Madison Square Garden promoter John Condon talked in nostalgic terms. McGuigan reminded him of Willie Pep. "McGuigan's trump card is that he never stops throwing punches." Willie Pep, now an Assistant Commissioner in Connecticut and regarded as one of the greatest featherweight champions of all time (he held the title for all but a four-month spell from November 1942 to September 1950), was impressed. McGuigan was "quick and strong," he said. "He never stops chasing. He gives the crowd a real fight. The way he keeps busy can win close fights. He has not only what it takes to be a World Champion, but potentially a really great one."

Promoter Bob Arum said that he had reservations about McGuigan but the Laporte fight had removed them. "He's now ready for any featherweight in the world."

Arum's Top Rank Incorporated match-maker Teddy Brenner described McGuigan as "a real breath of fresh air in a sport that thrives on new faces and attractions. He gives fans value for money, he gets into the ring to fight in every sense of the word. Definitely a star."

"The guy's a really talented fighter," said Mike Katz, boxing correspondent of the *New York Times*. "He showed he could really take a good punch as well as give one." Katz felt it was an expert piece of match-making by McGuigan's handlers, because Laporte was on the slide. McGuigan did his job well.

Associated Press writer Ed Schuyler was keeping a file on McGuigan, an honour he does not accord many European boxers. He felt McGuigan was putting in enough training to merit being watched. Too few top boxers have that sort of dedication, thought Schuyler. Schuyler said that McGuigan fought "American style." The sparring in Gleason's Gym had paid off ultimately.

* * * * * * *

4. Options

McGuigan's options were now extended. His performance in the ring against Laporte showed he was ready. Pedroza was accessible. Eastwood and Mickey Duff had shown their skills in the sharp world of boxing contracts. They were now to combine forces to land the big one — a world title shot. They could wait for a mandatory defence. But McGuigan was rated only third in the WBA charts, after Bernard Taylor.

He could make money in the meantime. Bob Arum, biggest of the three big promoters in the United States, offered 40,000 dollars to McGuigan to appear on the Marvin Hagler -v- Thomas Hearns undercard at Las Vegas a few months later. The opponents that were proposed were workhorse Americans, Tommy Cordova, Freddie Roche and Adrian Arreola.

The Eastwoods never even considered that option. They wanted a title fight. And they wanted Pedroza. They by-passed the option of dealing with Bob Arum and went to Santiago Del Rio, the Panamanian who manages Pedroza. Del Rio quickly sensed how badly Eastwood wanted the World title. He regarded Eastwood's ambition as an opportunity to make a lot of money.

Eastwood moved quickly. He discounted an offer from Frank Warren that would have involved a straight fight between McGuigan and Pedroza, 400,000 dollars for McGuigan, and a straight deal on fight options should McGuigan win.

Warren is a rival of Mickey Duff's. The two fight for dates on the London circuit in the same way as Duff ended Jack Solomons' monopoly of promotions in London. Warren was doing the same. The Eastwoods treated Warren's offer with contempt. They regarded it just as a publicity stunt. They doubted, in a BBC Grandstand interview, if Del Rio made any offer to Warren. Del Rio had his telexes of the offer. He was angered by the arrogance of the Eastwood line.

When Eastwood went to Panama to negotiate with Santiago Del Rio, so did Warren. Eastwood was welcomed by the Mickey Duff and Mike Barrett promotional organisation to promote in London. Warren, on the other hand, was an avowed rival of Duff's. The alliance between Eastwood and Duff was now at its peak.

The sticking point in the deal was options. Only Eastwood could offer these. Most boxing managers look for options. The idea is, that if you control a fighter and he loses the title, you can promote his first few defences of the new champion's crown. Boxing promoter-managers negotiate that as part of the terms of the title defence. Del Rio wanted options on McGuigan.

Eastwood would not tolerate this. He bought out the options, a wise move under the circumstances.

Del Rio demanded a purse of 600,000 dollars and expenses of 75,000 dollars tax free. He wanted 250,000 dollars or an option on McGuigan's first two defences, should he win, which Del Rio thought unlikely. When Eastwood paid over for the options, Del Rio was satisfied to accept. He felt Pedroza would retain the title anyway.

The week before McGuigan was to defend his soon-to-be-relinquished European title against Farid Gallouze, the deal was struck. The figures had just to be tied up.

Despite the fact that Pedroza was twenty-three pounds overweight, May 25 emerged as a likely date for the World title fight from the discussions in Panama.

Mickey Duff immediately moved into his role as salesman to the television companies. He quickly contacted all three networks. Mort Sharnik of CBS wanted a long run with McGuigan when he first took the Jose Caba fight.

They found that they could not take the championship fight when it came around. ABC, who specialise in title fights, also found May 25 unacceptable. NBC, whose buyer Dr Ferdie Pacheco was already sold on McGuigan, offered 440,000 dollars for the rights. It was big money for a defence against a European. Pacheco felt it was justified. Thus NBC were sold the rights for the fight before it was finalised.

The Eastwood approaches to Pedroza over the previous twelve months had never been approached with such zeal. Del Rio knew how badly this Belfast newcomer to management wanted his boxer to have a crack at the World title. He accepted an offer for Pedroza to attend a McGuigan defence of the European title against Farid Gallouze at London's Albert Hall, on February 23.

Pedroza was going to be there. Eastwood hoped the deal would be finalised.

* * * * * * *

5. Gentlemanly Conduct

The prospect of closing a deal with Pedroza made McGuigan's European title defence against Farid Gallouze in February more significant for the action off the ring than on it.

The chase for Pedroza had been proceeding for almost a year. Pedroza, the Eastwoods maintained, was purposely avoiding McGuigan. He opted for some easier defences rather than agree the big money terms being offered by the Belfast delegation that sent emissaries to coax him.

So to Farid Gallouze, a twenty-seven year-old perfume store manager, who was to offer a four minute and twenty seconds distraction in the midst of this soap opera.

The British Boxing Board of Control was unhappy that Gallouze had been nominated to compete for the title. They pointed to the previous experiences against Eguia and Ruan. Gallouze could do no better, they maintained.

Gallouze, a professional since October 1980, had been

unbeaten in his first eleven fights, but went to Holland and was beaten by Ray Somer and later lost to Belgian Jean Marc Renard, then European junior lightweight champion. He had won the French title at his second attempt — a points win over Philippe Martin. He also beat Luis de la Sagra. Renard and de la Sagra were names from the novice stages of McGuigan's career. It was back to that level.

The attendance was not bad, a 6,000 crowd that half-filled Wembley's indoor arena. Gallouze had sixteen wins and four draws in twenty-five fights. But he had all the appearances of a fighter who was going nowhere. What helped swell the attendance was a friendly soccer international between England and the Republic of Ireland at nearby Wembley outdoor stadium.

Still it was a shock to see Gallouze in tears. His manager explained why he had thrown in the white towel after just 260 seconds of boxing (almost 20p a second for those in the £50 seats). "I had to think of your wife and family," he explained.

McGuigan was telling him not to be upset, there was nothing to be ashamed of. It upset him that Gallouze was upset. The ringsiders were upset about their £50 down the drain. Worse was to follow when heavyweight Frank Bruno's opponent lasted less than a minute. The soccer fans were upset — they had been drenched by saxon rainfall, humiliated by saxon soccer stars, and had missed either the fight (if they had left the Stadium after the match) or an Irish goal (if they arrived in time for the fight). Some missed both. Others missed England's second goal as well.

McGuigan jabbed carefully through the first round, nothing ambitious, just pound, pound, pound on the Frenchman's body and face. Then came a combination. And the round ended.

"He was in there trying to take away the small section of the world that belongs to me," McGuigan said. "If they said I had to defend my title against Mahatma Ghandi I would fight him." Gallouze had been written off as fight number twenty-seven on the McGuigan trail.

But despite the routine victory, something was wrong. True, the fight had generated as much interest as many

CHASING A CHAMPION

World title fights in Wembley, the press officer Martin Corrie enthused. True, all the trappings were there: Rocky theme music, chants of *Barr-eee, Barr-eee,* (although you can only chant *Barr-eee, Barr-eee* for so long), a few cheers that got lost in the rafters rather than cascading back from the roof, and cheers for the ex-champions. Everybody clapped and cheered for John Conteh and saved up their boohs for Pedroza.

The man whose title McGuigan was seeking was not there. He was spared the fury of the crowd. He was back in his hotel bedroom.

Pedroza, his wife Rosa and manager Santiago Del Rio had checked into the Curzon House Hotel on Sunday morning. They caught a couple of hours sleep, attended an afternoon press conference "because it was good for the promotion," and went back to the hotel. What happened next was nothing. No further Eastwood contact, until Tuesday night.

Instead their London agent Pepy looked after them and brought them around London. He had no contact from the Eastwoods either, even as regards the financial arrangements.

At ten past seven on Tuesday they received a telephone call from an interpreter asking them to get a taxi to Wembley arena. They were incensed. They had come 6,000 miles to find they had to make their own way to the fight.

At eight o'clock, Stephen Eastwood arrived at the door of room 205. The interpreter was with him. Maybe my Spanish is faulty, he was saying. I was trying to tell you that the Eastwoods would collect Pedroza's party. Del Rio became even more angry.

Stephen Eastwood apologised for not having contacted the Panamanians since Sunday. Both he and his father, he said, were completely tied up with the business of the fight and they thought somebody else was looking after the visitors. Del Rio said he expected the Eastwoods to show some professional courtesy.

Stephen Eastwood feared that the World title fight deal was off. "No," said Del Rio. "But we're not going to tonight's fight."

That was that, until the fight was over, and the sleeping Del Rio was awakened by Mickey Duff and Mike Barrett. The dialogue resumed, Del Rio complaining that there was a lack of gentlemanly behaviour since they had arrived in London. "We are gentlemen," Duff answered. "You haven't behaved like gentlemen," Del Rio snapped.

And then the bargaining began. Money for options, money for expenses, the questions of tax on the purse and the possibility of fight dates (May 25 was found to be unacceptable, June 8 was discussed as a serious possibility) were debated. Outside in the foyer of the hotel a dozen more associates of the Eastwoods waited. At seven o'clock the word came out that a deal had been struck. The fight would definitely go ahead. The venue, although it was not announced, was almost certainly going to be an open air soccer stadium in West London, Loftus Road.

At 10.15 on Wednesday morning Del Rio and Pedroza and wife left London airport. They discovered they had to pay for the return part of their flight, 4,678 dollars, themselves. It was the final stage of the warfare between the fighters' camps that accompanied the striking of a deal.

The Eastwoods announced the deal at a press conference in a tiny bookshelved room in London's Holiday Inn. The first speech at the press conference was by Trevor McLintock. McLintock talked about how long he had known Barry, how he had teamed with him from the time he turned professional, sponsored his fights, how together with the Eastwoods the team had brought professional boxing back for the boxing public of Northern Ireland who had been starved of it for so many years so they could enjoy a little bit of normality, how one couldn't keep a good Irishman down, and how he was trying to overcome the problems encountered in encouraging Eusebio Pedroza to defend his title against Barry.

And how Smirnoff had brought Pedroza, his wife — his charming wife — and his manager, as their guests, to the fight.

"Unfortunately he wasn't feeling too well last night. That's the reason why he wasn't at the fight." The real reason? The Eastwoods would not comment. Everybody thought it was a downright insult, gamesmanship by Pedroza. Instead the Eastwoods described how they had negotiated until three in the morning, resumed at seven, in the morning, and signed a deal that went to twenty pages but still did not contain any date or venue. "Before July 10," the date was confirmed. "The location will be in London, but we haven't had the opportunity to assess the various venues."

"Santiago Del Rio," Stephen Eastwood complained, "turned out to be one of the hardest and most difficult bargainers that my father has ever met in business and he has been in business quite some time."

"These were the basic stumbling blocks: Pedroza wanted options of Barry's services if Barry were to beat him. We had to pay him, and pay him very dearly for these options. If Barry can beat Pedroza he will be a free agent."

Barney Eastwood told how he had spent thirteen hours negotiating with Del Rio in Panama, and wouldn't be happy until everything was settled "because he's a very difficult guy to work with."

Barry said it was absolutely fantastic, that this was the news he had been waiting for since the age of twelve "when I first took up boxing." Then he thanked in staccato turn "Mr Eastwood, Stephen Eastwood his son, my sponsor Trevor McLintock, match-maker Paddy Byrne, my family, my trainer Eddie Shaw, Mickey Duff and Mr Barrett," promoters of the Wembley venture and the ones who had cleared the way for Eastwood's promotion in London. "After their pulling it off I just hope I can pull it off."

McLintock assured the gathered press corps that "Pedroza and his manager would love to be here but unfortunately Santiago had a very big business meeting in Washington and sent his best wishes and apologies as he flew out at ten o'clock.

"I can't say it in Spanish, but that's the interpretation," McLintock said.

Three television cameras, two powerful heat-emitting lamps pouring white light on the top table, and fifty perspiring journalists recorded the event for posterity. The deal had been announced.

* * * * * * *

6. The Cost

Eastwood had no difficulty in attracting the television networks people to London. Out-of-States boxing was becoming a trend.

In the summer of 1985 boxing promoters began to look outside of America for venues. This was probably as a result of the difficulties created by television rights within America. Promoters needed television money to survive, but television reduced their attendance figures. Networks refused to black out telecasts in the area in which the fight took place. So promoters' only chance of cashing in on gate and television money was to get out of the United States. CBS took fights from Switzerland and Monte Carlo as well as Belfast.

Eastwood managed to promote in London without entering a bitter promotional war by siding with the bigger of the two parties vying for control of boxing in the English capital, Mickey Duff. The papers were told that this was solely an Eastwood promotion, but Duff is believed to have been in the promotion for a half share.

It was reckoned that the fighters would cost £1.1 million. Covering the pitch in the open air stadium cost £400,000. The promoters could get £250,000 (down from £400,000) for renegotiated television rights, £100,000 from sponsorship by Smirnoff, and the rest from the gate — people who paid from £20 to £100 for their tickets. The McGuigan cut from the world title fight was generally quoted to be £150,000. It may have been half of that again.

Paying for options is part and parcel of boxing wheeling-dealing. Bob Arum is one of the big three promoters who have come to dominate this end of the business. He thinks that Duff and Eastwood were wise, as someone who once paid 750,000 dollars to buy out three options when his fighter Davey Wall fought Japan's Tadashi Mahari for the World Junior Middleweight title.

"It was a shrewd move. Otherwise the Panamanians would have had them by the short hairs. A clever negotiator of boxing contracts like Duff would think of at least trying that. Duff knows all the right moves."

The long running story of negotiating the contract had a lucrative spin-off. The fight caught the imagination of the Irish public because of its high profile for six months. Both of Britain's main television channels ran half hour documentaries on McGuigan of the "leave the fighting to McGuigan" variety. Three jumbo jet loads of Belfast supporters travelled, thousands more from Dublin. Those from well-to-do gambling circles populated the ringside seats. Those on the terraces had travelled by train and boat for two days to be there.

For the two weeks before the fight, the McGuigan story led the sports pages in Belfast, Dublin and London.

This was to be the climax of McGuigan's career. Even McGuigan's handlers were surprised by the intensity of that climax.

* * * * * * *

7. Old Friends

Ireland ground to a halt when McGuigan won his title. Every bar with a television set was jammed with cheering customers. Wedding receptions and dances were interrupted by an exodus to find the nearest television set. People who had never shown the slightest interest in boxing were caught up in the spontaneous enthusiasm from the young boxer from Clones.

His former colleagues watched on their television sets. Efforts to bring Ken Buchanan down from Scotland failed when Buchanan could not be located. He confessed to an odd tear of joy when McGuigan won.

Martin Brereton, McGuigan's opponent in the six and a half stone Irish final of 1976, was supposed to be in London for the fight but his ticket fell through. He had got as far as Dublin airport when he got the bad news. Instead he made the fifty-mile dash home to Edenderry, County Offaly, to watch the contest on television.

Frank Mulligan was in London. Danny McEntee at home in Monaghan. They were both thinking of the twelve year-old they had met in Smithboro gym.

In New York, Bobby McQuillar, who had coached McGuigan in New York in 1983 and again before the Jose Caba fight in April 1984 told Rick Young that he felt McGuigan would win. "It's Barry's time," he said. "Pedroza's legs are getting old."

Young replied, "No, Bobby. I don't think it's going to go like that. It could go either way." Rick Young isolated himself in his living room to watch the boxers he had sparred. He was "ever so slightly in favour of Barry."

Vinnie Costello sat down in front of his set in Long Island. McGuigan's body punches would do it, he said.

McQuillar should have been in London to help McGuigan. He could not make it because of ill health. Instead he assessed the victory in his cold, clinical fashion at long distance:

"Continuous movement. That's what he needed to beat Pedroza.

"He hurt Pedroza a couple of times. You could tell. When he hit him he hurt him. You can't get hit on that liver and not get some sort of reaction — the biggest organ in your body. It don't take much pressure.

"It's hard to get over there, but he can do it. It's very hard to get on that side with the right hand. Lots of guys are scared to do it. Barry can just do that."

Rick Young felt beforehand that Pedroza had the edge in experience:

"McGuigan had the movement. He constantly moved for fifteen rounds. When the fight was over he was prepared to go five, ten, fifteen more rounds. His condition was superb.

"In the seventh I was quite surprised to see Pedroza go down. I think Barry caught him relaxing for a minute. He was lucky to get up. Barry had him on the edge several times. He was gone. I think he caught Pedroza off balance — you have to keep Pedroza off balance. His legs are getting older now. And when people get you off balance there's not much you can do. And that's what happened Pedroza.

"Pedroza was boxing good, moving and jabbing. The pressure Barry was putting on was phenomenal. Too many guys can't stand that type of pressure in a fight and Pedroza's legs were old."

The television people and the promoters were watching as well from New York. Mort Sharnik of CBS and promoter Bob Arum watched together. But they discovered by a quick canvass at an Irish bar later in the evening that McGuigan was still virtually unknown. True, boxing fans had heard of him. But even the Irish-American public were not responding with the enthusiasm of those at home.

Gerry Brown, boxing fan, watches all the cable shows. He watched from his home in Manhattan. "I made a lot of money on that Pedroza fight. Laporte should have had Pedroza's title. Man, he was cheated. I knew this boy McGuigan was going to be big when he fought Pedroza. He got such body shots. That's where the fights are won — inside. Fight fans in New York would go to see him if he ever came here.

"I gave this Irish guy in the office a hard time. I say to him who's the toughest guy in all Ireland. He say I dunno. I say Barry McGuigan. He say who's Barry McGuigan? I say you're no Irishman.

"Over here we don't go in for this white and black shit. We like a good fighter. Man, that McGuigan's a good fighter."

England too was enthusiastic about their new champion. Newspapers gave the fight saturation coverage: the *Sunday Mirror* made McGuigan's victory its front page lead.

"No one now," Hugh McIlvanney of the *Observer* declared, "is entitled to oppose very strenuously the claims some of us have made that this young man is the most dramatic fighter to emerge from these islands in half a century."

Patrick Collins of the *Mail On Sunday* applauded that "For fifteen rounds the fight had yielded everything we could have desired, teetering on a tightrope as two extraordinary fighters sought to impose their talent and authority. McGuigan was massive, inspired by the prevailing passion and by the prospect of the prize to be won, he offered a performance which will add his name to the litany of Turpin, Conteh, Buchanan and the rest."

"There was no doubting his victory," Ken Mays said in the *Sunday Telegraph*. "He piled up the points, and his thousands of supporters were ready for a ring invasion even before the final bell had sounded."

Nick Pitt told *Sunday Times* readers that McGuigan "proved that he not only had more desire than the champion, but significantly, more strength."

Alan Hoby of the *Sunday Express* declared it was the finest performance he had seen in a British ring since Randolph Turpin defeated Sugar Ray Robinson in 1951. "The twenty-four year-old Irishman, fighting out of his American-style crouch, came through against a world champion second only to Marvin Hagler in malevolence and menace."

Fred Bucombe said in the *News of the World*: "If he took a backward step, I didn't notice it. He attacked from the start and his pressure was relentless. For all of his twelve years in the ring Pedroza can rarely have been confronted by such a mass of energy."

McGuigan made the lead story in the *Sunday Mirror* where Bill Clark wrote "McGuigan's camp suspected that the freakishly tall Pedroza had trouble making nine stones and their tactic was to force him into a furious stamina sapping war. Scorning Pedroza's reputation as one of the all-time greats, McGuigan hounded him relentlessly."

Ireland's newspapers gave the fight saturation coverage. The *Sunday Tribune* pre-printed an eight-page colour magazine feature titled "Champion Of The World". The Sunday and Monday morning newspapers commented editorially on the success. Reporters were placed in various locations of the ground in London, in McGuigan's home town at Clones, and in Belfast.

From Clones they reported the fire that destroyed the family home and Barry's gym, built and equipped by his enthusiastic father many years before. (According to *Irish*

Times reporter Seamus Martin, when one of the family shouted "we're on fire" from an upstairs window, a drunken passer-by replied "sure we're all on fire tonight.")

The fire was to secure Barry's return to Clones earlier than was originally planned.

* * * * * * *

8. Press Conference

Up and coming boxers need the press to boost their careers. Champions keep the press waiting. Barry McGuigan kept journalists waiting for six hours in the Holiday Inn on Sunday morning. He arrived at 3.30, cheerful and smiling in the grand eloquence of the library room, microphones at his face, wife and child at his side. The family man was in town.

Blaine, the three year-old son, crept away to a corner and began to play with a telephone. Photographers swarmed around him in an ampitheatrical semi-circle. Barry looked tired, ever so slightly. He put back his head, relaxed and talked.

The headlines came from a statement that he would retire as soon as he was twenty-seven, or "twenty-seven and a half." "With my style you take a certain amount of punishment. An aggressive fighter is certain to get hit. This is too harsh a game to stay around in too long."

No, he had not reached his full potential. About seventy per cent. "I have a lot more to offer the people and I also think I have a lot more to learn. I was amazed I could go at such a pace for so long. I think I could have gone another five or ten rounds.

"The Pedroza fight taught me the value of patience, but I must work on being more polished, more accurate and finishing better with my main punches. My biggest asset is my strength. I must work on the finer points.

"One thing that annoyed me was that I could not pin him with more than one punch at a time. He was marvellously evasive. In the end, you know, I felt terribly sorry for him in a way. Standing there so dejected. A truly great champion having lost his title. He went out like a champion and a real man.

"The only time he really worried me for a moment was when he jarred me with a magnificent right-hander in the fourteenth. He never hit me actually harder than Laporte, but he hit me much more often."

To the horror of the image-conscious Eastwoods, McGuigan told a joke about a parish priest. But that did not appear in the morning newspapers. Another more printable witticism was about the fire: "I'd say they put it out with vodka . . . if there was any left."

He talked about his elbow ligament injury. He talked about the fighters he wanted to defend against in Belfast. He talked about not being able to floor Pedroza. He talked about his compliment, Pedroza had called him a great champion — "coming from him that was something special."

When did he realise he was World champion? Quick as a flash . . . "tomorrow night."

Eastwood talked about the bets that were laid in Northern Ireland on a McGuigan victory, and how he had laid a bet in Las Vegas, McGuigan to win, 14,000 to 10,000 dollars. Did the Irish object to the flag? Somebody wanted to know.

"We stand for peace," McGuigan said. "Leave the fighting to McGuigan." said Eastwood. But that did not appear in the morning newspapers.

* * * * * * *

9. Hero's Welcome

All that remained was the hero's welcome home. McGuigan was extremely tired when he made his way back on Monday past 20,000 cheering supporters in Belfast city centre, to the smaller crowd of about 4,000 in his home town, Clones. McGuigan was brought through the town on an open topped bus.

Two television crews swooped in helicopters over the town. Reporters from each of the Dublin, Belfast and London newspapers joined the celebrations in the Lennard Arms Hotel, owned by McGuigan's father-in-law, Jim Mealiff. Later in the week abandoned television cameras and radio links were bestrewn around the premises.

The banners had gone up in Clones ten days before the fight. One or two witty ones had started it all. The ordinary ones just said "Welcome to Barrytown" on the entrance routes and "Clones behind you Barry" at the exits. Then came the tongue in cheek ones, "take him to the cleaners" on the launderette, "We're banking on you, Barry" at the bank, "Be on your guard, Barry" at the police station, "In a flash, Barry" on the chemists, even one on the itinerants' site said "Scrap him Barry". Soon everybody had one.

On Thursday it was Dublin's turn. Dublin has been a disaster area for professional boxing. The police expected 25,000, something on the scale of receptions hosted for Olympic athletes. Over 100,000 came out.

Somebody on O'Connell Bridge waved his souvenir. A specially erected AA traffic sign pointing the way to "QPR Boxing" that he had taken home from London.

Lord Mayor of Dublin Michael O'Halloran mispronounced the nickname: the Clones Cyclops. McGuigan responded immediately: "It must be all the punches I've been taking."

* * * * * * *

10. Big Bucks

Just when McGuigan was on the threshold of something big in his amateur career, he became a victim of the politics of boxing. He is worried the same thing will happen in professional ranks. McGuigan's colleague on Eastwood's books, Hughie Russell, always maintains that amateur boxing is a cleaner game than professional boxing. "The only thing they fight about in professional boxing is money."

Now the prospect of big money looms before McGuigan. Lesser things have changed people's personalities.

McGuigan's financial arrangement with Barney Eastwood has always been the subject of speculation. Eastwood pays his big fighters well. Some of his lesser pugilists get paid £300 a fight, or £150 in cases. But Eastwood has looked after his loyal fighters with payments that come on time and are well handled by accountants to take account of tax benefits.

Yet the rumours trickled out from the camp that all was not well as regards the financial arrangements between Eastwood and McGuigan. In late 1984 McGuigan told a newspaper reporter from the *Sunday Independent* in Dublin that he was in the red. He had borrowed heavily to live in the years since he became a professional boxer. He had a mortgage on his house. He had to repay his father who had built the gym and kept him in times of low income. He had to pay his brother Dermot who had stayed in Clones even when the firm that employed him had closed down so as to support his brother in the vital times before the World title fight. He needed big money, and quickly.

McGuigan is said to have grossed £25,000 from each King's Hall promotion in Belfast. He is said to have earned £50,000 from the World title bout. Billy Costello, with whom many have compared McGuigan because he operated from a home-town base in upstate New York, Kingston, when defending his World Junior Welterweight title, earned just 25,000 dollars when he won his title in January 1984 in Texas.

McGuigan fought for very little money at the beginning, £5,000 for the first four or five fights. A reported £2,500 for winning the British title sounds much lower than the generally accepted £10,000. The figures that have been quoted as McGuigan's earnings range from the appallingly low to the ludicrously high, McGuigan claims that he is in the red. He also claims that he has never fallen out with B.J. Eastwood over money.

The bond between Eastwood and McGuigan is said to be the least susceptible thing in the maze of connections and friendships that now faces a great onslaught brought on by the presence of large tracts of cash within the family.

It is far more likely that the Eastwoods and the McGuigans will fall out over money, and to a certain extent the families are in danger of falling out among themselves.

Barry's father Pat and wife Sandra are the strongest influences on the boxer's financial dealings. McGuigan is certain to seek more money. More money means that Eastwood will have to stop promoting if he is to satisfy his boxer's demands. McGuigan will not be able to fight in Belfast and reap the cash rewards he demands.

The question of appearance money is also forcing McGuigan to think of abroad. His fees of £2,500 for an Irish appearance compare with soccer stars in the Irish team, top television personalities, and snooker champion Dennis Taylor. But the people who organised McGuigan appearances have not found them successful. Two showbusiness style promotions, one in Mullingar County Westmeath and the other in Drogheda County Louth were disasters. The Drogheda show was to have featured a video of the fight in a "Barry McGuigan experience", based on the tourist shows for London and New York. Like all the previous experiences of boxers dabbling in show business, the latest being Joe Frazier, it was a flop. A father who knows the world of showbusiness is not enough.

Barry's father Pat McGuigan, toured the United States in 1985 after his son's world championship victory. He called his group the Ringsiders, sang *Danny Boy* in the manner of the Loftus Road promotion, and also a new peace song called *Join Hands*.

He also called in on boxing promoters to chat. He learned and assessed just what McGuigan could make in New York. The promoters he met were enthusiastic.

John Condon in Madison Square Garden talked about a spectacular show with McGuigan and Puerto Rican Wilfredo Gomez topping the bill. That would involve the two major ethnic groups in New York City. It would earn McGuigan a million dollars.

Eastwood's only hope of raising that type of money would be in a closed circuit show of a McGuigan fight from Belfast. By piping the fight to cinemas all over Britain and Ireland and selling the television rights in America to ABC, Eastwood hopes to earn enough to appease McGuigan.

That was the start of the break-up of old associations. Eastwood and Mickey Duff fell out over money. Barney Eastwood and Stephen Eastwood fell out, publicly because Stephen Eastwood wanted a break from promoting after the Pedroza fight. Eastwood applied for a promoter's licence for his associate Al Dillon. In fact the relationship with Stephen Eastwood was a typical tempestuous father-son one, always fighting over the smaller aspects of the promotion, tickets, expenses, things like that.

Barry McGuigan fell out with Brian Eastwood, another Eastwood son who was handling McGuigan's publicity. The relationship between McGuigan and his personal manager was unclear to the advertising people who were interested in using McGuigan for endorsements in the aftermath of the World title fight euphoria throughout the summer of 1985. McGuigan's brother-in-law Dave Mealiff was an unofficial personal manager in this period.

The relationship between Eastwood and Duff was the most extraordinary of all. Duff was an old betting circles associate and friend of Eastwood's. He wanted McGuigan when the boxer was thinking of turning professional. He wanted to promote McGuigan in London. At one stage, Duff's deft handling had yielded four World champions based in Britain, Jim Watt, Paul Pender, Maurice Hope, and Charlie Magri. He became interested in McGuigan at the time of the European title fight and subsequently took charge of the television negotiations, and the deal to bring Pedroza to London.

In return he got to promote McGuigan's European title defences in London. At the first he insisted that McGuigan parade behind a Union Jack. The Eastwoods insisted on the blue flag of peace. Going back to Belfast having paraded behind a Union Jack would have eroded much of McGuigan's traditional support. Some felt that Duff was trying to force McGuigan into fighting outside of Belfast. Eastwood claimed afterwards that McGuigan would not fight in London again. When Angel Mayor failed to appear in Belfast in October they began to suspect that Duff was attempting to sabotage the Belfast promotions again. In fact the attempted saboteurs came from farther afield.

The break between Eastwood and Duff was not made of such sinister stuff. But they did get back together to allow Eastwood to strike a deal with Bob Arum, the biggest of the New York promoters.

Eastwood had one card up his sleeve before he entered negotiations. He knew that ABC were prepared to pay "just under 400,000 dollars" for a McGuigan defence in Belfast. He knew that September 28 was free, and had already signed Herrol Graham to fight for the European middleweight title against Ayub Kalule in Belfast as an undercard fight on that date. He had examined the possibilities of a closed circuit deal.

Television companies, because they pay the major contribution towards a promoter's expenses, have a lot of clout. They can change a venue or a challenger by indirect means. The ABC people told Eastwood that they would prefer McGuigan -v- Taylor to be in Belfast for what they called the "McGuigan crowd scene."

So Eastwood met Duff at a press conference in New York announcing Hagler's defence of the World middleweight title against Duff's boxer, John Mugabi. Afterwards they adjourned, with Arum, to the tenth floor office of Arum's on Third Avenue. They continued talking at the Manhattan Cafe on the corner of 64th Street and First Avenue. The talks resumed on Tuesday morning in Arum's office. The deal was announced before lunch-time.

Eastwood was prepared to pay 250,000 dollars with premiums of 50,000 dollars for London and 120,000 dollars for Belfast. There was little doubt that Belfast was to be the venue.

The Eastwoods told the Irish and British press that they were not signing Taylor but were working on a voluntary defence with Chilean Juvenal Ordenez. They said that Earls Court in London and the National Exhibition Centre in Birmingham were likely venues. Earls Court was already booked for an exhibition on that date.

11. White Hope

Bob Arum is the latest in a long line of big time American promoters. He believes that boxing in America is in a recession, not a depression. From his tenth floor office in a modern fifty-storey block simply called 919 Third Avenue he has organised Hagler-Duran, Hagler-Hearns, and Hagler-Mugabi fights, the nearest things to super-fights the sport has had to offer over the past two years.

He rarely meets a fighter. He looks after promotions, television, press, tickets, and money. He talks to managers who talk to fighters. He likes the manager from Belfast who struck a deal with him over the Taylor fight that leaves Taylor the highest paid title challenger in featherweight history. He wants McGuigan to fight in New York.

"McGuigan in New York will come sometime next year. I have never met McGuigan but I have now met Eastwood and I got on fairly well with him. I would like to promote McGuigan in New York. He would be a tremendous attraction.

"I don't think his appeal would be limited to Irish people. He is a colourful kid. He is an attractive fighter. I know he would be a big attraction in Las Vegas as well as New York. People are already asking me about Caeser's Palace.

"Salvador Sanchez was a very exciting featherweight. But I think Barry McGuigan being who he is could certainly be the most dynamic of all the featherweights yet."

When the contract for the Bernard Taylor fight was being agreed there was no question of options. "They realised I am sophisticated enough not to agree to it," Bob Arum says. "When McGuigan fought for the title he was not the number one challenger. Taylor is."

Even within a week of his winning the WBA Featherweight title, McGuigan was named at number three in terms of marketability in world boxing.

Marvin Hagler, recently deed-polled Marvellous Marvin Hagler, was a specialist media boxer, exciting to watch, exciting to listen to. He specialises in retreating to his gym in Provincetown, near Boston, and re-emerging feeling "real mean." He can claim seven figure purses.

Larry Holmes, the only heavyweight around with any

stature (the only body that recognises him as World champion is the body with least stature, the International Boxing Federation or IBF) is a survivor from Muhammad Ali days and has an undefeated record that was comparable with Rocky Marciano.

McGuigan was twenty-four, heavily in debt, but one of only two white champions around (the other is WBA light-welterweight champion Gene Hatcher). He was also Irish, fighting from Northern Ireland with a peacemaker tag, and did not have to resort to an image of the ex-criminal for his appeal.

Old time promoters got the formula right. They played on people's prejudices, trying out fights between black and white (Jack Johnson -v- Jim Jeffries), bum -v- hero, American -v- foreigner, well to do -v- poor. Promoters like George Tex Rickard, who promoted the Jeffreys-Johnson fight and others for twenty-five years up to 1930 could pack 100,000 in to see his promotions.

Big gates are no more, but boxing promoters managed to stay afloat as each new development was utilised to help their sport, films, picture magazines, radio, network television, closed circuit television and finally American cable television. Closed circuit television made Floyd Patterson rich. Network rights helped Muhammad Ali make fifty-seven million in a twenty-year career. An exclusive contract with ABC helped make Sugar Ray Leonard even richer.

To reach Sugar Ray Leonard dimensions, McGuigan needs to become a white hope. "Now he is champion. He has finished the first phase. He needs to consolidate his position. He needs to have three or four fights that everyone knows he is going to win. He is lucky he is in a division that has so much talent." NBC commentator and former buyer Ferdie Pacheco is probably the biggest McGuigan fan in the circles of power in New York.

Getting bigger than NBC, CBS, and ABC means cable television. Home Box Office, or as it appears in the long sheets of daily American television listings, HBO, is a subsidiary of Time-Life International. They tend to buy eight to ten fights a year. They show all their fights in prime time, the evening, and all of them have to be very, very good.

The volume of boxing is better on the networks. They tend to have fighters on before the cable gets them. But when HBO get interested, they pay more than the networks. Within weeks of McGuigan's victory, they were exploring the possibilities of getting one of his fights. The networks can outbid HBO for some prime time fights, simply by passing on the extra fees to their advertisers in extra costs. But HBO pride themselves on being able to pay a particular amount for a particular event, and show it with no television commercial breaks between rounds. They heard about a McGuigan -v- Wilfredo Gomez match. They were interested. In New York, an up-and-coming Irishman against a Puerto Rican household name means big bucks.

HBO claim McGuigan can be very big, that he is not big now, but it takes a little while. "He has to be shown in prime time. He has not got that exposure yet, just in the afternoons. He has a lot going for him. He is an excellent fighter, he has a great personality. And the Pedroza fight swayed a lot of people, even a lot of people who do not have much interest in boxing."

Image means far more to cable television than the quickfire, stop-for-the-Krispies-commercial world of network broadcasting. They like to do pieces on boxers, variety pieces, so their subscribers will be informed. But TV is about action and events, even in the world of piped television. As soon as McGuigan -v- somebody is an event, HBO will be chasing for a killing. It's hard to sell documentaries.

Boxing is going through a down period at the moment, Alex Wallec of ABC complains. All coded ratings are down, sport has saturated the mind of the US television viewer, and the sport has no charismatic superstar. It is not a depression, just a recession, he maintains. The public is confused by the profusion of champions. Nobody has captured the general imagination of the sport. McGuigan has a chance.

"There is a combination of three things going for him.

Because of this he could become a truly great fighter.

"His talent as a fighter is not the most important factor.

"The fact that he is white means people will root for him for racist motives, people will root for him because they can identify with him, and people will be constantly reacting positively to Barry."

Bobby McQuillar, the coloured boxer from Michigan who coached McGuigan in the American ways, has heard it all before. "Yeah, alright, alright, let's have the white hope. So what. If boxing needs a white hope, bring him on. It's got another one. What the hell. Let's bring some life back into the game."

* * * * * *

12. Home Town

In Clones the McGuigan family is now learning to cope with fame. McGuigan goes shopping and he is mobbed. Loss of privacy troubles his wife, Sandra. But McGuigan maintains that since he comes from a home which already has a showband singer in residence and a grocery store out front, fame is not a problem.

Dermot, Barry's brother, and his father Pat, contributed more to the champion's success than the handlers in Belfast or London or New York. They answered reporters' questions and queries throughout McGuigan's career. Television crews were entertained.

Dermot never boxed, perhaps fearing comparison with his famous brother. Instead he plays golf so well that his handicap of three puts him in contention for all the top Irish amateur competitions.

The presence of such fame and fortune places great strain on the aspect of McGuigan's background that appeals most to those whose job it will be to sell him to America. The settled Irish family will have to be very settled to cope with the pressure of having a World champion in the clan.

In the meantime, in an effort to direct the money generated by this success back to McGuigan, the family have begun to sell souvenir items connected with his boxing.

Whatever happens in the arenas of New York, the family will live in a small town with small town pride.

Whether McGuigan can achieve his ambition to make as much money as possible in three and a half years and stay in Clones remains to be seen. Funny things happen on the way to the championship.

APPENDIX 1

Boxing: The Medical Facts

"I am aware of one thing, that this is too harsh a game to mess around in for too long."
— Barry McGuigan at his post World Championship press conference.

From the time he turned professional, McGuigan vowed to give up boxing as a career before his twenty-eighth birthday in February 1989.

In doing so he betrayed his mistrust for the sport he loves. It is a mistrust he shares with many other great boxers. Muhammad Ali said once that he would not like his son to box. McGuigan would not like his son Blaine to box either, although the toddler has a pair of toy boxing gloves he got as a present from a relative at home. Juan Laporte, who made the difficult decision to retire at twenty-five after being hurt by McGuigan, would sympathise. So too will Alan Minter, once fined £300 as an up-and-coming for not being aggressive enough in a fight against Jan Magdziara and whose later opponent Angelo Jocopucci died as a result of injuries received in the ring.

The overriding danger in boxing is brain damage, a conclusive catalogue of evidence compiled over fifty-seven years. McGuigan tries not to think about the prospect of brain damage. He says that he is, nevertheless, conscious of it.

Boxing always has had a sordid reputation. It was outlawed until the development of the Chambers-Queensberry rules in 1867, and boxers who killed an opponent could be charged with manslaughter until 1929. Charges were brought against National Sporting Club officials in 1901 after the death of Murray Livingstone. They were acquitted when the jury was persuaded that what had happened was an accident.

In May 1928, Dr Harrison Martland, a New Jersey pathologist, told the New York Academy of Medicine that punch-drunkeness most often affected boxers of the slugger type, who took considerable head punishment seeking only to land a knockout blow. The first sign was some slight mental confusion. The second was "a peculiar mental attitude characterised by hesitancy in speech, tremors of the hands and nodding movements of the head," while in severe cases there was a peculiar tilting of the head, tremors and marked mental deterioration.

Martland estimated that fifty per cent of veteran professional fighters had the condition in either mild or severe form.

He quoted Gene Tunney on his decision to retire soon after being dazed for two days from a punch during a sparring session in preparation for the 1928 heavyweight fight with Jack Dempsey. "I want to leave the game that has threatened my sanity before I met with an accident in a real fight with six inch gloves that would permanently injure my brain."

Martland was debunked by a 1954 survey by Drs Harry A. Karplan and Jefferson Browder. They claimed that the derogatory remarks about punch-drunk fighters were only based on popular theory. They gave 1,043 boxers electro-encephalograms (EEGs), a test that records patterns of electrical activity in the surface aspects of the brain. Sluggers and skilfull fighters rated the same. Kaplan, as a ringside physician, claimed most punches missed their mark anyway. Defenders of boxing still cite this study.

In 1957, neurologist MacDonald Critchley examined sixty-nine cases of chronic neurological disease in boxers and agreed that many were examples of punch-drunk boxers. He found the condition more common in professionals than in amateurs, in sluggers than in stylish fighters, and in the second rate or third rate boxers rather than a contender for a championship title. He stated that "the sum total of contests is important as well as the number of occasions upon which the boxer had been rendered unconscious." He found that, on average, punch-drunkeness developed sixteen years after a boxer began his career.

Dr Fra McCown, a ringside physician, wrote in 1955 that the notion of punch-drunkeness was "a medical cliche with which to label any boxer whose performance and behaviour in or out of the ring was unsatisfactory and abnormal."

In the 1960s, the deaths of Charlie Mohr (whose ill-fated defence of his NCAA championship caused boxing to be dropped as an intercollegiate sport) and Danny Moore, who had misled Californian authorities about his medical record, reopened the debate on boxing.

In 1962, a *Journal of the American Medical Association* report suggested less padding in the gloves, so the prospect of injuring ones fists would deter from hard blows. Eight ounce gloves as opposed to six ounce gloves, allow harder punches and lessen the damage to the hands. But it has been argued that six ounce gloves can inflict more damage.

In 1969, A.H. Roberts studied 224 retired professional boxers, selected at random. He found seventeen per cent had evidence of brain damage in the form of drooling, unsteady gait, and memory loss. Others showed "disturbed neurological functions."

Psychiatrist John Johnson, published a report in the *British Journal of Psychiatry* in 1969 and found that sixteen out of seventeen subjects he examined were suffering from conditions such as chronic amnesia, morbid jealousy, undue rage reactions or outright psychosis. He also used a new technique of injecting air into the brain before taking an X-ray and found a pattern of celebral atrophy in ten out of seventeen, which showed that half the men in the sample were missing brain tissue. Brain cells, damaged in a boxing match, never regenerate.

In 1973 Dr J.A.N. Cornellis, a British neuropathologist performed autopsies on the brains of fifteen former fighters who had died of natural causes. There was a pattern of celebral atrophy in fourteen of the fifteen.

Cornellis found that boxing damage is worst deep in the

middle of the brain, and also in the cerebellum, the outer section near the back of the head. The deep regions regulate short term memory. As brain tissue atrophies, the ventricles, the vessels in the brain filled with spinal fluid, grow larger. The worst cases have a cavum septum pellucidum, a cave in the septum, a literal hole between the ventricles, two to eight millimetres wide. Muhammad Ali was discovered to have this condition in 1981.

The cerebellum is the region that regulates muscular coordination and balance, will cause slurring of speech and a subject may appear to stagger if he is damaged here. Cornellis later told a BBC radio debate: "If the head is struck, it's reasonable to assume that what is inside it will be damaged."

The year after Cornellis's study, a British middleweight was diagnosed as being punch-drunk. He was only twenty-five!

The development of CAT scans has produced three more studies in the 1980s, all producing further evidence of damage to brain tissue in boxers. Last year Dr George Lundberg editorialised in the *Journal of the American Medical Association*: "every knockout is acute brain damage. Acute brain damage is common in boxing and occasionally kills regardless of medical treatment."

Eye specialists have voiced concern as well. Dr Weve of Utrecht, an authority on retinal detachment, said that boxing was not a sport but "a very brutal show for people with a minimum of heart and brains and a maximum of infantile atavism." The highest paid boxer of his era, Sugar Ray Robinson, retired suffering from a detached retina. Other eye injuries common to boxers include vitreous opacity, paralytic diplopia, iritis, glaucoma and cataract.

The case of Muhammad Ali was the most famous of all. Ali announced his retirement in December 1981 saying: "I don't want to be one of them old fighters with a flat nose saying 'duh-duh-duh' before a fight."

Afterwards on television, when asked if he might have suffered brain damage from his twenty-one-year ring career Ali replied: "It's possible."

Four years beforehand, in 1977, Dr Ferdie Pacheco, a general practitioner who had known Ali since 1962, quit working his corner. "He took some mammoth beatings. If you spent twenty years in boxing and an equal amount of time in medicine, you could see brain injury coming up.

"There were the fights with Frazer, Foreman and Norton, to say nothing of all the sparring with Larry Holmes and Michael Dokes. They were not ordinary sparring partners. They are now heavyweight champions of the world.

"A moron could add up the picture of impending brain damage, and I urged him to quit because I didn't think it would be wonderful to have the most joyful talented guy in the world stumbling around and mumbling to himself. But he was the one who wanted to stay on stage. The only role he knew was being champion. I'd just as soon have been wrong."

When Ali announced a return to the ring in April 1980, even his father Cassius Clay Senior, protested. "He wasn't sure of his speech. That boy has been at it since he was twelve years old. A man can only stand so many licks to the head."

Muhammad Ali was beaten in October by Larry Holmes, after getting a clean bill of health from a doctor despite signs of a "speech disorder". Later in England, when interviewed on BBC radio, he slurred his speech, and when he recited a poem on how he would beat Holmes in a rematch, most listeners found it incomprehensible. The BBC cancelled the broadcast of a taped interview for another programme because Ali's speech was too slurred to be understood.

Ali counter-attacked: "When you get as great as me, people are always looking for some type of downfall.

"People say I talk so slow today. That's no surprise, I calculate I've taken 29,000 punches. But I earned fifty-seven million dollars and I saved half of it. I may talk slow, but my mind is okay.

"Why are they picking on boxing? It's because the black men are so superior in boxing that they want to stop it. Well, the black man's so hungry, he's got to fight."

Recent fatalities have shown that headgear does not work. There are no easy ways out. According to Dr George Lumberg, *JAMA* editor: "either boxing should be abolished or blows to the head should be made illegal."

"I'm a grown man," Randy Tex Cobb told *Sports Illustrated* magazine when they wanted to give him eurological tests in 1982. "If a man doesn't want to fight, then lay down sucker. I'm not going to have someone run my life for me. I'm a whore who sells his blood instead of his ass. But that comes with the sport."

Cobb fought Holmes for the world title in 1981. He took such a bad beating that ABC TV commentator Howard Cosell declared that he would never broadcast a professional boxing match again.

* * * * * * *

The debate of course will go on. Those against boxing compare it with gladiatorial contests, with cock-fighting (which has already been banned) and point to casualty figures:

— 360 cases of boxing deaths in forty years.

— Undeniable evidence of brain damage among boxers, massive loss of brain tissue that does not regenerate, cavities in the brain tissue itself, loss of memory and loss of control of vital muscles.

They will also criticise the motives of the sport:

— Boxers try to effect the most damage on the opponent's head that they can manage, to knock each other out. Men are paid money to punch each other on the head.

— The British Boxing Board of Control issue licences to men to carry out this violence.

— The Board punishes and reprimands boxers for not being violent enough.

— The activity, glorifying violence, is degrading for both participants and spectators.

— A report by a Canadian sociologist in 1983 claims that, far from appeasing violent traits in boxing spectators the sport encourages them. People are more likely to commit

acts of violence after watching boxing.
— It is not possible to clear a man on medical grounds as fit to take an unspecified number of blows to the head.
— The money involved makes it profitable for boxers and promoters to ignore medical directives, and for matchmakers to pair up unequal opponents.
— The prime motive among spectators is not scientific punching in most cases, but knockouts and blood.

Defenders of boxing compare it favourably with much more aggressive sports, sports with higher incidence of serious injury, like rugby or American football, or adventure sports like mountaineering, hang-gliding, skiing, and deep-sea diving. It can readily be compared with fencing, a similar combat-based sport, where the defensive clothing can be accidentally pierced, as happened one world champion.

They argue:
— Boxing is strictly controlled, that each boxer must have a clean bill of health and if the British Boxing Board of Control or similar promoting body is not satisfied, the bout will not be allowed to go ahead. (This happened a major contest on the bill when McGuigan won the world title.)
— That these medical controls have been stepped up further since Young Ali managed to avoid having a weak skull and an artery defect in his head detected.
— That controls also mean that any boxer who has been knocked out cannot box again for ? ? ? ? days.
— That boxers, like jockeys or grand prix drivers, enter the sport of their own free will, are granted certain safety standards, and are aware of the dangers.
— That the emphasis in boxing on defence, rather than attack, denies that it is glorified violence.
— That the benefit of the sport is greater than the drawbacks. Young kids, who might have stolen cars or become street brawlers, learn to discipline their aggression and spend their fury in the boxing ring.
— That it offers an opportunity for ghetto kids, from the wrong end of society (formerly Irish and Italian, now Black and Hispanic) to achieve fame and fortune and be-

come millionaires. For many more it offers at least dreams of doing so.
— That boxing, legal or illegal, would carry on anyway. If it was banned it would be impossible to control.
— That the matching of boxers is strictly monitored so that only fighters of equal weight and ability meet.
— That boxing is an industry, with employment, with money and careers involved, and with a mammoth reputation for entertainment value.

WORLD-WIDE RING DEATHS
(Amateur and Professional)

Year	Deaths	Year	Deaths	Year	Deaths
1918	1	1941	4	1964	15
1919	1	1942	5	1965	7
1920	1	1943	3	1966	9
1921	2	1944	2	1967	4
1922	3	1945	6	1968	6
1923	1	1946	14	1969	5
1924	1	1947	11	1970	7
1925	6	1948	14	1971	5
1926	4	1949	18	1972	11
1927	1	1950	11	1973	3
1928	4	1951	12	1974	5
1929	9	1952	17	1975	5
1930	10	1953	22	1976	7
1931	3	1954	8	1977	3
1932	0	1955	10	1978	9
1933	6	1956	11	1979	4
1934	2	1957	8	1980	6
1935	1	1958	9	1981	5
1936	6	1959	11	1982	7
1937	2	1960	10	1983	9
1938	3	1961	10	1984	4
1939	1	1962	14		
1940	4	1963	10		

APPENDIX 2

Champions

WORLD FEATHERWEIGHT CHAMPIONS
1889   Ike O'Neill Weir (Ireland)
1890   Torpedo Billy Murphy (New Zealand)
       Young Griffo (Australia)
1892   George Dixon (Canada)
1897   Solly Smith (USA)
1898   Dave Sullivan (Ireland)
       George Dixon (Canada)
1900   Terry McGovern (USA)
1901   Young Corbett II (USA)
1904   Jimmy Britt (USA)
       Brooklyn Tommy O'Sullivan (USA)
1906   Abe Atell (USA)
1912   Johnny Kilbane (USA)
1923   Eugene Criqui (France)
       Johnny Dundee (USA/Italy)
1925   Louis Kidd Kaplan (USA/Russia)
1927   Benny Bass (USA/Russia)
1928   Tony Canzoneri (USA)
       Andre Routis (France)
1929   Battling Battalino (USA)
1932- Disputed by Tommy Paul, Kid Chocolate,
1937   Freddie Miller, Alberto Arizmendi, Mike Belloise,
       Petey Sarron
1937   Maurice Holtzer (France)
       Henry Armstrong (USA)
1939   Joey Archibold (USA)
1940   Harry Jeffra (USA)
1941   Joey Archibold (USA)

Albert Wright (Mexico)
1942 Willie Pep (USA)
1948 Sandy Saddler (USA)
1949 Willie Pep (USA)
1950 Sandy Saddler (USA)
1957 Hogan Bassey (Nigeria)
1959 Davey Moore (USA)
1963 Sugar Ramos (Cuba)
1964 Vincent Saldivar (Mexico)

WBC TITLES
1968 Howard Winstone (Wales)
     Jose Segra (Cuba/Spain)
1969 Johnny Famechon (Australia/France)
1970 Vincente Saldivar (Mexico)
     Kuniaka Shibata (Japan)
1972 Clemente Sanchez (Mexico)
     Jose Legra (Cuba/Spain)
1973 Eder Jofre (Brazil)
1974 Bobby Chacon (Mexico)
1975 Ruben Olivares (Mexico)
     David Kotey (Ghana)
1976 Danny Lopez (USA)
1980 Salvador Sanchez (Mexico)
1982 Juan Laporte (USA/Puerto Rico)
1984 Wilfredo Gomez (Puerto Rico)
     Azumah Nelson (Ghana)

WBA TITLES
1968 Paul Rojas (USA)
     Shozo Saijyo (Japan)
1971 Antonio Gomez (Venezuela)
1972 Ernesto Marcel (Panama)
1974 Ruben Olivares (Mexico)
     Alexis Arguello (Nicaragua)
1977 Rafael Ortega (Panama)
     Cecilio Lastra (Spain)
1978 Eusebio Pedroza (Panama)
1985 Barry McGuigan (Ireland)

EUROPEAN FEATHERWEIGHT TITLE HOLDERS

1912	Jim Driscoll (Britain)
1913	Ted Kid Lewis (Britain)
1919	Louis de Ponthieu (France)
1920	Arthur Wyns (Belgium)
1922	Eugene Criqui (France)
1923	Edouard Mascart (France)
1924	Charles Ledoux (France)
	Henry Hebrans (Belgium)
1925	Antonio Ruiz (Spain)
1928	Luigi Quadrini (Italy)
1929	Knud Larsen (Denmark)
1929	Jose Girones (Spain)
1935	Maurice Holtzer (France)
1938	Phil Dolhem (Belgium)
1939	Lucien Popescu (Romania)
1941	Ernst Weiss (Austria)
1942	Gino Bondavalli (Italy)
1945	Ermanno Bonetti (Italy)
1947	Al Phillips (Britain)
	Ronnie Clayton (Britain)
1948	Ray Farmechon (France)
1953	Jean Sneyers (Belgium)
1954	Ray Famechon (France)
1955	Fred Galiani (Spain)
1957	Cherif Hamia (France)
1958	Sergio Caprari (Italy)
1959	Gracieux Lamperti (France)
1962	Alberto Serti (Italy)
1963	Howard Winstone (Britain)
1967	Jose Segra (Spain)
1968	Manuel Calvo (Spain)
1969	Tomasso Galli (Italy)
1970	Jose Legra (Spain)
1973	Gitano Jiminez (Spain)
1975	Elio Cotena (Italy)
1976	Pedro Nino Jiminez (Spain)
1977	Manuel Masso (Spain)
1977	Roberton Castanon (Spain)
1981	Salvatore Melluzzo (Italy)

1982 Pat Cowdell (Britain)
1983 Loris Stecca (Italy)
     Barry McGuigan (Ireland)

BRITISH FEATHERWEIGHT TITLE HOLDERS
1895 Fred Johnson
1897 Ben Jordan
1900 Will Curley
1901 Jack Roberts
1902 Ben Jordan
1905 Joe Bowker
1906 Johnny Summers
     Jim Driscoll
     Johnny Summers
     Frank Spike Robson
1907 Jim Driscoll
1913 Ted Kid Lewis
1915 Llew Edwards
1917 Charlie Hardcastle
     James Tancy Lee
1920 Mike Honeyman
1921 Joe Fox
1924 George McKenzie
1925 Johnny Curley
1927 Johnny Cuthbert
1928 Harry Corbett
1929 Johnny Cuthbert
1931 Nel Tarleton
1932 Seaman Tommy Watson
1934 Nel Tarleton
1936 Johnny McGrory
1938 Jim Spider Kelly
1939 Johnny Cusick
1940 Nel Tarleton
1947 Ronnie Clayton
1954 Sammy McCarthy
1955 Bill Spider Kelly
1956 Charlie Hill
1959 Bobby Neill
1960 Terry Spinks

CHAMPIONS

1961 Howard Winstone
1969 Jimmy Revie
1971 Evan Armstrong
1972 Tommy Glencross
1973 Evan Armstrong
1975 Vernon Sollas
1977 Alan Richardson
1978 Dave Needham
1979 Pat Cowdell
1982 Steve Simms
1983 Barry McGuigan

APPENDIX 3

The Irish Champions

Eleven generally recognised World champions in six divisions were born in Ireland. Three bareknuckle champions were also born in Ireland.

PETER CORCORAN arrived in England as an unbeaten Irish heavyweight where he met Colonel O'Kelly, a gambling gentleman. O'Kelly is credited with having bought Bill Darts when Corcoran won a 1771 championship contest in less than one minute. Corcoran later beat Ned Turner and Sam Peters. He lost his title in twenty-eight minutes to Harry Sellers in 1776.

DUGGAN FEARNS won the title back for Ireland in 1779 against Harry Sellers at Slough. It lasted less than a minute and the fight was said to be a fix. Fearns, the "Irish boatswain", dropped out of sight and was never heard from again.

PADDY RYAN was born in 1853 in Thurles, County Tipperary. He weighed fourteen stone, four pounds, and won the American heavyweight title in 1880 by defeating Joe Goss in eighty-seven rounds at Collier Station, West Virginia. In 1882 he was beaten by John L. Sullivan in nine rounds for 5,000 dollars a side. Sullivan beat Ryan twice subsequently.

Other great Irish bareknuckle fighters were:

DAN DONNELLY born in 1788, the first Irish champion

and the only bareknuckle boxer to be knighted (at a banquet by the Lord Lieutenant). He beat English champion George Cooper in eleven rounds at a natural ampitheatre in the Curragh of Kildare later to become known as Donnelly's Hollow. He died at the age of thirty-two, one of his long arms is said to be preserved in a public house in Kilcullen.

SIMON BYRNE born in 1836, was once tried for manslaughter after Sandy McKay died as a result of injuries sustained in a forty-seven-round contest in London. Byrne later fought for the title against Jem Ward in 1833 and died as a result of a fight that lasted ninety-nine rounds against James "Deaf" Burke in 1833: a three hours and sixteen minutes affair.

NED O'BALDWIN born in Lismore in 1840, fought in England and America, where he once served eighteen months for violating the law by fighting Joe Wormwald.

YANKEE SULLIVAN was born James Ambrose in Cork in 1813, fought Tom Hyer for the title and 10,000 dollars a side in 1849 and lost in sixteen rounds.

JOE COBURN was born in County Armagh in 1835 and drew great battles against Ned Price and Jem Mace.

MIKE McCOOLE was born in Ireland in 1837 and beat Bill Davis for the American title in 1866. Lost a decisive match with Tom Allen for the World bareknuckle title in 1873.

JIM DUNNE born in Kildare in 1842, beat Jim Elliott and Bill Davis in American championship bouts.

JOHN MORRISSEY born in 1831, beat John C. Heenan for the American title in 1858, and later became a congressman and senator.

JIM ELLIOTT born in 1838, won American heavyweight title from Bill Davis in 1867, was sentenced to sixteen years in prison in 1870, and eventually lost to John L. Sullivan in an 1882 glove contest.

JACK DEMPSEY born near Clane in 1862, his real name was John Kelly. He adopted the name Dempsey to keep his ring career secret from his family. His first professional fight was in April 1883, when he knocked out Ed McDonald in twenty-one rounds at Long Island, and in July of the following year, in his fifteenth fight, he won the World middleweight title by knocking out George Fulljames in twenty-two rounds at Great Kills, New York. Dempsey was nicknamed "Nonpareil", and over the following five years he retained his title with knockout wins over Jack Fogarty, George La Blanche and Johnny Reagan. In 1889 he was knocked out in thirty-two rounds in a return with La Blanche, but as the Canadian had achieved the feat by using the illegal backhand "pivot" blow, Dempsey kept his title. He made another successful defence in 1890, beating Australian Bill McCarthy in twenty-eight rounds in San Francisco, but in January 1891 he was finally deposed when Bob Fitzsimons knocked him out in thirteen rounds in New Orleans. He died at Portland, Oregon in 1895.

JACK McAULIFFE born in Bantry in 1866, he emigrated to America when only fifteen years old, and on July 1, 1884 he began one of the most remarkable careers in boxing with a three-round win over Bob Mace in New York. In February 1886 he won the American lightweight title by beating Jack Hopper in seventeen rounds and claimed the vacant world title, as did the English champion Jem Carney. In November 1887 the two met at Revere, Massachusetts. The bout was declared a draw when the rival supporters invaded the ring in the seventy-fourth round. For a time both continued to claim the world championship. Carney, however, returned to England and didn't fight again for nearly four years and when, in October 1888, McAuliffe knocked out Billy Dacey in eleven rounds in New Jersey, the Irishman won more or less universal recognition as champion. His only other official defence was in September 1892, when he knocked out Billy Myer in fifteen rounds in New Orleans. He retired in 1894, but came back for four more bouts in 1896 and 1897. McAuliffe finished his career with a record of forty-one wins, nine draws and three no-decisions in his fifty-three fights. Only two other world champions were never beaten throughout their careers: Rocky Marciano and Jimmy Barry (bantamweight champion 1897 to 1899). McAuliffe died at Forest Hills, New York in 1937.

IKE O'NEILL WEIR born in Lurgan in 1867, the "Belfast Spider" began his professional career in Manchester in 1885 but emigrated to America a year later and settled in Boston. By the end of 1888 he had lost only one of his twenty-eight fights. After a third round knockout win over Jack Beck, he was matched with Frank Murphy for the vacant world featherweight title at Kouts, Indiana in March 1889. The bout was declared a draw when police intervened in the eightieth round. When the by-now overweight Murphy returned to England and refused to meet Weir again, the Irishman won considerable — though not universal — acceptance as champion. His claim lasted a mere ten months before New Zealand born but Australian based "Torpedo" Billy Murphy knocked him out in fourteen rounds in San Francisco. He wasn't beaten again for over four years — in 1893 he knocked out the by-then ex-champion Murphy in six rounds — but in March 1894 he suffered only the third defeat of his career when beaten in three rounds by Young Griffo and promptly announced his retirement. He died at Charlestown, Massachusetts in 1908.

DAVE SULLIVAN born in Cork in 1877, he launched his professional career with a sixth round knockout of Frank Stone in New York just after his seventeenth birthday. In October 1897 he was outpointed over twenty rounds in London in a bout given partial recognition as being for the world bantamweight title. He then moved up a weight, and in September 1898 he took the world featherweight title when champion Solly Smith broke his arm and had to retire in the fifth round at Coney Island. A mere forty-six days later he was disqualified in the tenth round against George Dixon at New York's Lennox Athletic Club. Thereafter Sullivan lost almost as often as he won, and he retired after being knocked out in nine rounds by Kid Herman in 1905. He died in 1929.

GEORGE GARDNER born in Lisdoonvarna in 1877, he began fighting in 1897 and lost only two of thirty-five fights up to the end of 1901. In October 1902 he was outpointed over twenty rounds in San Francisco by Jack Johnson. In July of the following year — after a first round knockout of Galwayman Peter Maher in Boston — he won the World light-heavyweight championship by knocking out Jack Root in twelve rounds at Fort Erie. Just over four months later he lost his title when outpointed over twenty rounds in San Francisco by Bob Fitzsimons, who thus became the first man to win world titles at three different weights. Thereafter Gardner fought mainly as a heavyweight and he retired in 1908 after being beaten in seven rounds by Tony Ross. He died in Chicago in 1954.

JIMMY GARDNER brother of George and born in Lisdoonvarna in 1885, he began as a lightweight in 1902 and in December of that year had the first of a famous series of five fights with Mike (Twin) Sullivan. Two years later he was outpointed over twelve rounds by Jack Blackburn. Gardner moved up to welterweight. In April 1908 he was beaten in twenty-five rounds in a title fight with the by-then champion Sullivan in Los Angeles. Six months later, after Sullivan had given up the title through weight difficulties, the Clareman won partial acceptance as champion by outpointing Jimmy Clabby in New Orleans. Three weeks later he drew with Clabby in the same city. He afterwards boxed as a middleweight and retired in 1912 after being knocked out in three rounds by Frank Klaus, who a year later won the world title. Gardner died in Boston in 1959.

TOM McCORMICK born in Dundalk in 1890, he joined the British army and began boxing while stationed near

Plymouth in 1911. By the end of 1913 he had lost only two out of thirty-eight fights. He left the army and went to Australia. In January 1914 he won the British and Empire (now Commonwealth) welterweight titles by outpointing Johnny Summers over twenty rounds in Sydney. A fortnight later he won European recognition as world champion by beating Dane Waldemar Holberg on a sixth round disqualification in Melbourne. The following month he defended his three titles with a first round knockout of Summers in Sydney, but in March, just fifty-six days after he became champion, he lost his titles by a twenty round decision to Englishman Matt Wells. He rejoined the British army at the outbreak of World War I and was killed in action in France in 1916.

MIKE McTIGUE became a professional in 1909, when aged only seventeen, and spent over ten years as a journeyman fighter in small towns throughout Canada and the northern United States. In 1921 he graduated to New York, where a points win over Jeff Smith gained him considerable prestige and attention. Late the following year he took off on a four-fight tour of England and then, on St Patrick's Day 1923, he won the world light-heavyweight title by outpointing Battling Siki over twenty rounds in a Dublin cinema. The following October McTigue retained his title in a controversial ten-round draw with Young Stribling in Georgia. In May 1925 he was deposed in a fifteen-round decision in New York by Paul Berlenbach. Outpointed by Tommy Loughran in a fight for the vacant title in 1927, McTigue fought on for another three years and suffered four first-round knockouts — before the New York State Athletic Commission withdrew his licence at the age of thirty-eight.

JIMMY McLARNIN born in Belfast in 1906, his family emigrated to Canada ten years later, and at the age of fourteen he was spotted by Pop Foster. Foster trained McLarnin for three years before launching him as a professional. Within eighteen months of his debut Baby Face McLarnin was one of the best lightweights in the world. In 1928 he was outpointed in a world title challenge by Sammy Mandell. He moved up to welterweight where he quickly became the top attraction of the first half of the thirties. First round knockouts of Sid Terris, Phil McGraw and Sammy Baker (as well as a second round demolition of Ruby Goldstein) made McLarnin a sensation, and in 1933 he won the world title in a record two minutes and thirty-seven seconds from Young Corbett III. In 1934 and 1935 he lost, regained, then finally lost his title in three classic fifteen-rounders with Barney Ross, and he retired in 1936 after a ten-round victory over reigning lightweight champion Lou Ambers. McLarnin is accepted as one of the true all-time greats, and his popularity with the public made him perhaps the largest fortune amassed by any boxer in the pre-World War II era. He fought twenty-three fights against fourteen men who either were or later became world champions, and of his last ten fights, only one was against a non-champion. He and Foster had a legendary father/son-like relationship, and when Pop died in 1956 he left his entire fortune of 286,000 dollars to McLarnin. He now lives just outside Los Angeles.

JOHNNY CALDWELL born in Belfast in 1938 and a bronze medallist in the 1956 Melbourne Olympics, he turned professional in 1958 and inside two years won the British flyweight title by knocking out Frankie Jones in three rounds in the King's Hall. In May 1961, after Frenchman Alphonse Halimi had won European recognition as world bantamweight champion by outpointing another Belfastman Freddie Gilroy in a fight for the vacant title, Caldwell outpointed Halimi at Wembley. Five months later he repeated the win at the same venue. The following January, in a fight for the undisputed title with Brazilian Eder Jofre in Sao Paulo, Caldwell was beaten in ten rounds. In October 1962 he lost a memorable battle with Gilroy at the King's Hall, two years later he won the British bantamweight title by stopping George Bowes in seven rounds. He lost his title to Alan Rudkin in ten rounds in March 1965 and retired after one more bout.

RINTY MONAGHAN born in Belfast in 1920, made his professional debut when only fourteen-and-a-half, knocking out Vic Large in four rounds. By the middle of 1938 he'd notched up twenty-one straight wins. He suffered his first defeat when knocked out in five rounds by Jackie Paterson in Belfast. His career was interrupted by his service in the British army during World War II. In May 1945 he resumed fighting and the following July made his only appearance south of the border when outpointing Joe Collins in Dublin. In October 1948 he won NBA (forerunner of the WBA) recognition as world flyweight champion by outpointing Dado Marino in London in a fight sanctioned as a world title bout in the twenty-six counties, and the following March he won universal acceptance as champion by knocking out Paterson in seven rounds. Monaghan defended his title twice. He beat Frenchman Maurice Sandeyron on points and drew with England's Terry Allen. He retired as undefeated champion in April 1950.

APPENDIX 4

Irish-American World Champions

HEAVYWEIGHT
John L. McElligott	1882-1892
James J. Corbett	1892-1897
Jack Dempsey	1919-1926
Gene Tunney	1926-1928
James J. Braddock	1935-1937

In the era of Jack Johnson's reign as heavyweight champion, three Irish-Americans won the racially restricted "White Championship":

Luther McCarthy	1913
Arthur Pelkey	1913-1914
William (Gunboat) Smith	1914

LIGHT-HEAVYWEIGHT
Philadelphia Jack O'Brien	1905-1910
Jack Dillon	1914-1916
Tommy Loughran	1927-1929
Jimmy Slattery	1927 and 1930
Billy Conn	1939-1941

MIDDLEWEIGHT
Mike O'Dowd	1917-1920 and 1922
William Bryan Downey	1921
Jock Malone	1922-1923
Harry Greb	1923-1926
Mickey Walker	1926-1931
Freddie Steele	1936-1938
Paul Pender	1960-1961 and 1962-1963

WELTERWEIGHT
Paddy Duffy	1888-1890
Mysterious Billy Smith	1892-1894
Matty Matthews	1900-1901
Honey Mellody	1906-1907
Mike (Twin) Sullivan	1907-1908
Jimmy Clabby	1910-1911
Jack Britton	1915, 1916-1917 and 1919-1922
Mike Glover	1915
Mickey Walker	1922-1926
Tommy Freeman	1930-1931
Freddie Cochrane	1941-1946

LIGHTWEIGHT
Jimmy Goodrich	1925
Lew Jenkins	1940-1941
Sean O'Grady	1981

JUNIOR-LIGHTWEIGHT
Steve Sullivan	1924-1925
Frankie Klick	1933-1934

FEATHERWEIGHT
Terry McGovern	1900-1901
Tommy Sullivan	1904-1905
Johnny Kilbane	1912-1923
Dick Finnegan	1926-1927
Joey Archibald	1938-1940

BANTAMWEIGHT
Tommy (Spider) Kelly	1887 and 1899
Hughey Boyle	1887-1888
Jimmy Barry	1894-1899
Terry McGovern	1899-1900
Harry Forbes	1902-1903
Frankie Neil	1903-1904
Jimmy Walsh	1905-1907
Johnny Coulon	1910-1914
Joe Lynch	1920-1921 and 1922-1924